Tell Us What Happened

Tell Us What Happened

Michelle Robb

Scirocco Drama

Tell Us What Happened
first published 2023 by Scirocco Drama
An imprint of J. Gordon Shillingford Publishing Inc.
© 2023 Michelle Robb

Scirocco Drama Editor: Glenda MacFarlane
Cover design by Doowah Design
Author photo by Gaetz Photography
Production photos by Ian Jackson (Epic Photography)

Printed and bound in Canada on 100% post-consumer recycled paper.
We acknowledge the financial support of the Manitoba Arts Council and

The Canada Council for the Arts for our publishing program.

Production inquiries to:
telluswhathappenedplay@gmail.com

Library and Archives Canada Cataloguing in Publication

Title: Tell us what happened / Michelle Robb.
Names: Robb, Michelle, author.
Description: A play.
Identifiers: Canadiana 20220492786 | ISBN 9781990738227 (softcover)
Classification: LCC PS8635.O23 T45 2023 | DDC C812/.6—dc23

J. Gordon Shillingford Publishing
P.O. Box 86, RPO Corydon Avenue, Winnipeg, MB Canada R3M 3S3

To the women in my life,

to Edmonton,

to radical empathy,

to my parents, my siblings, Gavin,
Andrew, Katherine, and Callie.

Never underestimate the impatience of the oppressed.

Michelle Robb

Michelle Robb is an actor, dancer, and playwright from Amiskwaciwaskahikan/Edmonton. Her formal education was at the University of Alberta, where she completed two years of their BA Drama Honours program before graduating their BFA Acting program in 2021. Her dance training has taken place at a handful of Canadian studios, as well as the ImpulsTanz Festival in Vienna, Austria. She is an alumna of the Citadel Young Playwriting company, where she wrote *Tell Us What Happened* in 2017 before it went on to win the Novitiate Award in the Alberta Playwriting Competition in 2020. Michelle's independent work in dance and playwriting has been funded by the Edmonton Arts Council and the Canada Council for the Arts.

Acknowledgements

Tell Us What Happened began as a class assignment five years prior to its publication, and throughout that time I've accumulated many debts. The following is an incomplete list of people in my life whose support is unquestionably laced into the fabric of this story.

Thank you to the original production team, many of whom stayed committed to the project throughout a two-year marathon of pandemic postponements. I would like to especially acknowledge the contributions of Lora Brovold, Betty Hushlak, and Ben Franchuk—their expertise and rigour were a vital component of the production's success.

Thanks to my former playwriting classmates, Jonah Dunch and Matt Gwozd. My writing roots will always trace back to the curious energy of our first writers' table.

To Callie Lissinna, thank you for a delightful friendship held together through humour, discipline, and passion.

To Katherine Coker, the world is lucky to have you and I'm even luckier to be your friend.

To my deeply supportive parents, Brent and Irene Robb, I love you endlessly and I would give you the world if I could.

And finally, my deepest gratitude to Heather Inglis, without whom this play simply would not exist. Thank you for teaching a class that made me fall in love with plays, and for your unwavering commitment to this story from the moment I pitched it. Although I am credited as the writer on this script, I will always regard it as the product of our collaboration. Thank you for believing in me.

Playwright's Note

In 2017, I set out to write a play that featured an ensemble of girls who are clever, wild, and flawed. I was a twenty-year-old undergrad student with a mild social media addiction, an imbalanced ego, and a deep sense of confusion over how to navigate the murky waters of high stakes gossip—if I wasn't in on the hearsay, I might find myself on the "wrong side" of some social alliances. Meanwhile I felt conflicted when I overheard things like "Can you believe she knows what he did and she's still friends with him?" or "She knows what her son did, and she's done nothing about it."

It's tempting to collapse nuance when we're afraid and confused. I fall into that trap all the time and of course social media only catalyzes that tendency. We must find a way to embrace complexities without compromising the survivor's voice and healing process. Most of us know someone who has committed an act of sexual violence. Rapists are not necessarily hooded figures in dark alleys, they're our friends, relatives, classmates, co-workers, and partners. There is no gold standard for how a woman is supposed to respond upon learning that someone close to her is not who she thought he was. If she decides to keep her relationship with him after learning what he's done, that is probably one of the toughest decisions she's ever made and if we respond by turning on her, I fear we're missing the whole point. We mustn't let the discomfort of these realities tempt us into dragging each other down. Perhaps we have a deeper responsibility to build a stronger world through empathic relationships that hold space for respectful disagreements and emotional exposure. Unfortunately, it's pretty tough to discuss these matters sympathetically because rage is an appropriate reaction to history and some aspects of the current legal system—how can we simultaneously presume innocence and believe the victim?

I don't know all the answers to the questions in this play, but I believe humans are capable of changing the world through hard conversations, and I do believe those changes are a-coming. *Tell Us What Happened* has filled my early twenties with laughter, joy, and learning. I hope future production teams enjoy living in the clubhouse as much as I do.

Foreword
By Heather Inglis

The journey of a play from inception to stage is usually an odyssey rife with blood, sweat, tears, reversals of fortune, narrow escapes, and plenty of dramatic irony.

Tell Us What Happened started humbly in 2017 as a class project in a writing program I pioneered: the Citadel Theatre Young Playwrights' Company.

Early in Michelle's work on this play, I knew I wanted to produce and direct it. Producing a student's work is, of course, exceedingly rare for any theatre educator. But Michelle's characters have fresh, realistic, urgent voices that drew me in. She writes about young women who are smart and flawed and fully human colliding in a complicated scenario: a perpetrator of harm is someone they love. The characters in *Tell Us What Happened* are drawn from the experiences of the playwright. Michelle was part of a community that was thinking hard about the struggles of young women and how they could be supported in a world that still treats them as expendable and dismissible.

As Michelle began drafting the earliest writing that would become the play, #MeToo hit like a tsunami, placing into sharp focus the myriad of ways women had been abused. At this galvanizing moment in history, sexual assault was the subject of both the mainstream media and everyday conversation. As women stood together and told the truth, the sheer magnitude of the culturally sanctioned sexual violence towards us was revealed. There was strength in our numbers. The internet had ignited a revolution. And with the revolution, we saw men in our communities, men we knew, men we trusted, face the irrevocable consequences of their callous mistreatment of women.

Although *Tell Us What Happened* was written at the precise moment mass consciousness about sexual violence was changing, the play is set before #MeToo. Michelle weighed what was happening and smartly opted to tell her story in a world where characters do not have the influence of a global awakening to aid them in the messy business of negotiating relationships in the wake of a sexual assault. In their world, the issues of the play are an uncharted frontier forcing them to struggle with the very nub of a situation for which there are no good answers. Setting the play prior to #MeToo, enables it to ask fearless questions of the post-#MeToo era, urging us to confront the uncomfortable places where who we love and what we know collide.

Theatre has always asked audiences to consider difficult scenarios for which there are no easy answers. In this tradition, *Tell Us What Happened* invites audiences to grapple with a hair-raising scenario none of us would ever wish to live, from the safety of our theatre seats. It offers us a window into a set of circumstances that challenge easy assumptions about how sexual assaults play out and who the perpetrators are.

What do we do when people we love do inexcusable things? Do we sever ties and cut people out of our lives and communities? Do we have a deeper responsibility to build a better world through our relationships with them? In a world where perpetrators of sexual assault often evade consequences, what can we do to assist survivors to get justice? The internet, like fire, is a powerful tool. It can reveal the truth and it can obscure it, leaving a path of human destruction in its wake. What are the costs of seeking justice on our own terms when the tried-and-true methods of public accountability fail?

This is a play of questions; the conversations it evokes compose its final act.

Tell Us What Happened was originally scheduled to be produced by Theatre Yes in May of 2020 but was postponed indefinitely due to the COVID-19 pandemic, breaking the hearts of the artists involved. In 2020, the play won the Novitiate Award at the Alberta Playwriting Competition. It was then rescheduled between waves of the pandemic and postponed again.

Five years after the play was first conceived during a defining moment of cultural change, a pandemic, two postponements, and twelve drafts later, the world premiere of *Tell Us What Happened* finally hit the stage May 2022, a coproduction between Workshop West Playwrights' Theatre and Theatre Yes. A child of the cultural storms it was created in, this is a work that does not simplify complicated issues into headlines or memes, but rather offers audiences an invitation to examine difficult emotional and moral questions. It is an optimistic work. It trusts that we are both intelligent and compassionate and that we can find our way through the most difficult circumstances with careful thought, open hearts, and the support of our friends, colleagues and loved ones.

Heather Inglis
November 2022

Production History

Tell Us What Happened premiered on May 12, 2022 at Workshop West Playwrights' Theatre in Edmonton, Alberta, with the following cast and creative team:

Cast

CHARLIE .... Bonnie Ings

ZOEY..Michelle Diaz

PIPER .... Gabby Bernard

LEAH .... Jameela McNeil

JOSH.. Matt Dejanovic

Creative Team

Director...Heather Inglis

Assistant Director...Lora Brovold

Stage Manager ....Betty Hushlak

Set Design... Brian Bast

Multimedia Design ....Ian Jackson

Sound Design... Kiidra Duhault

Costumes & Lights.. Whittyn Jason

Charlie (Bonnie Ings) and Josh (Matt Dejanovic) chatting with Piper (Gabby Bernard) before they go out shopping. Photo by Ian Jackson at Epic Photography.

Leah (Jameela McNeil) continues her post in "Tell Us What Happened." Photo by Ian Jackson at Epic Photography.

Charlie (Bonnie Ings) confronts Josh (Matt Dejanovic) and tells him about what's going on in her secret Facebook group. Photo by Ian Jackson at Epic Photography.

Zoey (Michelle Diaz) trying to persuade Leah (Jameela McNeil) to go out for a night on the town. Photo by Ian Jackson at Epic Photography.

Charlie (Bonnie Ings) and Josh (Matt Dejanovic) trying to hang out in spite of everything. Photo by Ian Jackson at Epic Photography.

Charlie (Bonnie Ings) walks in on Piper's (Gabby Bernard) breakdown. Photo by Ian Jackson at Epic Photography.

Charlie (Bonnie Ings) receives a phone call while hanging out with the girls (Jameela McNeil, Gabby Bernard, Michelle Diaz). Photo by Ian Jackson at Epic Photography.

Leah (Jameela McNeil) sends the email to Josh's practicum school with the support of the other girls (Michelle Diaz, Gabby Bernard, Bonnie Ings). Photo by Ian Jackson at Epic Photography.

Characters

CHARLIE: 21 years old. Leader and founder of the secret online girl group, "Tell Us What Happened." Best friends with Josh. Friendly and funny. Wise but nonetheless still young.

ZOEY: 23 years old. "Tell Us What Happened" administrator. Leah's cousin. Smart, boisterous, and sensitive. Not as strong as she makes herself appear.

PIPER: 21 years old. "Tell Us What Happened" administrator. Intuitive, bright, shy until you get to know her. Often underestimated by her peers.

LEAH: 17 years old. Member of "Tell Us What Happened." Zoey's cousin. Sweet, brave, and eager. Admires the other members of the group. Loads of courage.

JOSH: 22 years old. Best friends with Charlie. He has a handful of close guy-friends, but he can't be himself around them the way he can with Charlie. Charismatic, friendly, clever. Aspiring teacher about to finish his Education degree.

Setting

Autumn, 2015.

A happily cluttered living room in a rental house shared by Charlie, Piper, and Zoey. Fairy lights along the walls, a couch with colourful blankets, and a flag with all the gender symbols. The room is sprinkled with books, pipes, art supplies, records, and pride flags. Ugly, abstract paintings that are cute in a weird way are either on the walls or stacked around the room. The whole place looks like an incomplete art project. This is The Clubhouse.

The set for the original production at Workshop West Playwrights' Theatre featured the living room and kitchen; however, the show can be performed just in the living room. The original production used projections and multimedia to create the world of the internet during the Facebook posts.

Notes on the Text

These characters think fast and talk fast. They're all pretty smart and they know each other really well. These familiarities are evident in the momentum of their dialogue. Moments and pauses must be earned. The chatter of this play should emulate the cadence of a girls' locker room.

This script uses slash notation to indicate the start of the next line.

Capitals usually indicate volume. Italics indicate some form of heightened intensity, but not necessarily volume.

The actor playing Zoey can change the name of the fish every night.

A spotlight on LEAH. She speaks what she is posting in the online secret group, "Tell Us What Happened."

LEAH: Content Warning: Sexual Assault, and maybe rape?

I've never posted anything in here, but I just really need to get this out. Sorry if it's rambly. I've already typed and deleted this like, six times and I don't really know where to start.

I think I was raped a couple months ago. But I just need you guys to tell me if this was actually rape or if it was just me being stupid...

Lights fade on LEAH and up on The Clubhouse.

Evening. PIPER sits on the floor, laptop open, making a craft with tin foil, masking tape, and newspaper. CHARLIE is holding a container of cashews soaking in water.

CHARLIE: I'm not being stupid! It makes cheese!

PIPER: It's not cheese, it's cashews in water!

CHARLIE: But if you soak them for 24 hours, then put them in a blender and add the nutritional yeast, it becomes a substance that *looks* like cheese and *tastes* like cheese—

PIPER: —but *isn't* cheese. I'm all for experimenting but at the end of the day we should call it what it is.

CHARLIE: Lasagna.

PIPER: *Vegan* lasagna. Therefore, it's not cheese. It's weird, blended nut water.

CHARLIE: Just wait till tomorrow and you'll be all about the "weird blended nut water."

PIPER: Hey, did you see Leah's post?

CHARLIE: I was reading about it online and tons of people make it.

PIPER: *Charlie.* Did you read Leah's post in the group?

CHARLIE: Leah Madison?

PIPER: Do you think maybe someone should check on her?

CHARLIE: *(Checking her phone.)* Hold on...

PIPER: You should text her.

CHARLIE: Oh my god, Leah...

PIPER: She should come over, right?

CHARLIE: Well, I'm heading out right away.

PIPER: I thought you were staying to watch *Pirates.*

CHARLIE: I'm going shopping with Josh to help him get something for Julia.

PIPER: Is he really incapable of getting his girlfriend a birthday present without your input?

CHARLIE:	Believe me, I asked him. And she's not his girlfriend yet, so he's worried about overdoing it with a gift.
PIPER:	He should make her something.
CHARLIE:	Yeah, right! That guy's hands have the agility of like, two loaves of bread.
PIPER:	But it would be *nice*. I used to make stuff for Andre all the time.
CHARLIE:	Piper, you've *got* to forget about Andre.
PIPER:	He liked my art.
CHARLIE:	But Andre is also an artist, unlike Josh.
PIPER:	So what's he gonna get her?
CHARLIE:	No idea. Did you text her?
PIPER:	I messaged her but she hasn't seen it yet.
CHARLIE:	So text her.
PIPER:	My phone died.
CHARLIE:	So charge it.
PIPER:	I lost the charger.
CHARLIE:	You *still* haven't found it?
PIPER:	I just have to clean my room and then I'm sure I'll find it!
CHARLIE:	I'll text her then. She could even sleep over if she wants.
PIPER:	Tell her I'm gonna watch *Pirates* tonight.
CHARLIE:	I don't think she cares about *Pirates*.

PIPER: Just tell her.

CHARLIE: Piper, I love you, but there are more important things to say to Leah right now than tonight's Netflix lineup.

PIPER: Just tell her I'm watching / *Pirates of the Caribbean*.

CHARLIE: *Pirates of the Caribbean*, I know but—

PIPER: *(Looking out the window.)* Josh is here.

CHARLIE: Shit, I'm not even ready yet.

>   *CHARLIE waves to JOSH, then finishes typing her message to LEAH. PIPER retreats to her craft.*

CHARLIE: Kay, there. I told her you're watching *Pirates*.

PIPER: But did you tell her I'm watching *Curse of the Black Pearl*?

CHARLIE: Does it matter?

PIPER: It's the best one.

CHARLIE: *(Going to her room.)* I gotta grab my purse.

>   *JOSH enters.*

JOSH: Yo! 'Sup, Piper?

PIPER: Oh, you know. Movie night.

JOSH: Hey, I watched that documentary you recommended about those mountains in Peru.

PIPER: Venezuela. Aren't they cool?

JOSH: Super cool! It's on my bucket list for sure, like someday, yennow? Whatcha makin'?

PIPER:	A centaur.
JOSH:	Cool, like that dude in *Harry Potter*.
PIPER:	Yeah, him.
JOSH:	Sweet! That'll go great with your last project. Where is your last project?
PIPER:	It's in my closet next to the uhh, but no I just—no yeah I have to finish it bt—
JOSH:	It was looking super cool.
PIPER:	I ran out of key chains.
JOSH:	I've got some key chains at home if you need more. Like, old ones from camp and stuff. I could bring them over if you want?
PIPER:	Oh cool yeah okay because then I could—
CHARLIE:	*(Re-entering.)* Hey, sorry. I just gotta find my wallet. *(To PIPER.)* Have you seen it?
PIPER:	I thought it was on the table.
JOSH:	Is it the one you're holding?

It is.

JOSH:	Every time.
CHARLIE:	Shut up.
PIPER:	Did Leah respond?
CHARLIE:	*(Checking her phone.)* ...She's asking which *Pirates* movie you're watching.
PIPER:	Tell her *Curse of the Black Pearl*.
JOSH:	Nice! That's the best one.
PIPER:	Thank you!

JOSH: Seriously, the last one sucked.

PIPER: You just can't go wrong with the original.

JOSH: No shit. I hate when producers keep making bad movies as a part of a series. Like, *Shrek*? Shoulda stopped at one.

CHARLIE: Okay / the second one's cute.

PIPER: But the baby Shreks in the third movie?

JOSH: It was a one-hit wonder if you ask me.

CHARLIE: *(Sarcastic.)* You mean you don't like *Shrek the Halls*?

PIPER: Can you guys believe *Shrek* came out fourteen years ago?

JOSH: No way that's true.

CHARLIE: *Fourteen* years ago?

PIPER: Yeah, the first one came out in 2001 and it's 2015, so like, / math!

JOSH: Math.

CHARLIE: Why do I suddenly feel old?

JOSH: Speak for yourself, I refuse to let *Shrek* define my age.

PIPER: Is Leah coming over?

CHARLIE: Yeah, she said she'll come in an hour or so.

PIPER: Oh good. Zoey should be home by then.

JOSH: Leah...?

CHARLIE: Madison. She's a friend of ours. Zoey's cousin.

JOSH: Oh her! She's in my Drama 111 class.

CHARLIE: Yeah, she's having a rough time though, so she's gonna sleep over.

JOSH: I was about to say, yeah. She hasn't been to Drama in like, over a month. She even missed our midterm.

CHARLIE: I still can't believe you're taking first year Drama.

JOSH: I needed another Arts credit!

CHARLIE: Mr. "I graduate this year."

JOSH: Whatever, dude. Drama's easy. You just play games and stuff. And as long as you raise your hand every time someone does a piece and call it "interesting" or "visceral," your grade spikes right up.

CHARLIE: Well Leah needs that course. I had no idea she stopped going to her classes.

JOSH: I even messaged her last Friday to see what's going on but she never replied. Anyway, we should get going.

CHARLIE: (On their way out.) Where are we going, anyway?

JOSH: We're gonna go to Richmond and look around there.

CHARLIE: Any idea what you wanna get her?

JOSH: Nope! That's why you're coming.

CHARLIE: 'Bye, Piper!

JOSH: Later, dude!

PIPER: … 'bye…

JOSH and CHARLIE leave. PIPER stares at the door. She opens her laptop. Spotlight on PIPER as she comments on Leah's post.

PIPER: I'm so sorry that happened to you. I'll see you later tonight. If you don't mind my asking, who was the guy?

CHARLIE makes a post in "Tell Us What Happened."

CHARLIE: Hello my lovelies. I just wanted to pop in say how much I love you all, seeing how today marks three years of "Tell Us What Happened." When I originally made this group, I thought maybe, like 20 people would join, so 438 members is beyond anything I dreamt of three years ago. So thanks. Hope to see all you locals at the anniversary party next month!

Remember, if you ever have any concerns about the group, feel free to message me, Zoey Davidson, or Piper Watson.

I love you each.

Charlie.

Shift. LEAH sits on the couch. Curse of the Black Pearl *has just ended. PIPER is in the kitchen.*

LEAH: What time is Zoey supposed to be home?

PIPER: *(From offstage.)* I have no idea. She was out shopping. But she also mentioned a party so who knows.

LEAH: Do you think she's going with Dallas?

PIPER: *(Entering with gummy worms.)* Probably. She won't stop raving about him.

LEAH:	And she still "doesn't even like him."
PIPER:	"We're just friends!"
LEAH:	"He just listens to all the same music as me, and besides / he's like a brother!"
PIPER:	*"He's like a brother!"* Seriously! Unless you fuck your brother on a casual basis—
LEAH:	Ew, Piper!
PIPER:	Sorry.
LEAH:	*(Checking her phone.)* Have you been reading the other comments on my post?
PIPER:	My phone died and I lost the charger.
LEAH:	Use mine. Here. *(Goes to her bag.)* So you haven't seen them?
PIPER:	Not since I asked about the guy.
LEAH:	Right, well it's kind of overflowing a bit. Like, five other girls are saying that he did something similar to them.
PIPER:	*What.*
LEAH:	Not like, what he did to me—thank god—but like, sounds like he's no stranger to crossing the line.
PIPER:	*(Reading the post.)* Goddamn…Anika… Haley…Paige…Jenny…Quinta…GABBY?
LEAH:	Right?
PIPER:	How would Gabby even *know* him? She lives in BC.
LEAH:	She said it happened in high school. Do you think Charlie's seen this?

PIPER: Doubt it. She's out shopping.

LEAH: Lindsey commented and said I should go to the police, but like—I don't know...

PIPER: Well did you—like the day after it happened—did you like, go to the hospital?

LEAH: I was in shock. Like, maybe I should've but I thought it was my fault—

PIPER: It's not your fault—

LEAH: I didn't even think to go to the hospital—I totally should've!

PIPER: Hey, you were probably super hungover and really freaked out and stuff, plus like, the last thing you'd wanna do after a night like that is lay on a table while some nurses stick a bunch of stuff up your—

LEAH: Yeah don't the kits, like, really hurt?

PIPER: YEP. And then they get added to the mountains of other ones to be "processed" and then who's to say if they'd even get to yours before it expires—

LEAH: Ew.

PIPER: I know, right. So maybe you dodged a bullet by not going to the hospital.

LEAH: But Lindsey thinks I should go to police, but like, I don't know.

PIPER: Well the police would want some sort of evidence—but who's to say! We don't have to get into details now.

LEAH: I was so scared to post this. I didn't think people would believe me.

PIPER: We'd believe you no matter what. I just don't want to tell Charlie.

LEAH: I don't want to tell *Zoey*.

PIPER: Oh my god! She doesn't know?

LEAH: She's been out with Dallas all day!

PIPER: Oh god, she's gonna freak!

LEAH: And I don't even wanna think about Charlie.

PIPER: I just don't want Zoey to yell.

              The front door bursts open. ZOEY parades into the room, her hands full of shopping bags.

ZOEY: I'M HOME!

PIPER: Zoey!

LEAH: Hey, Zo!

ZOEY: You guys would not *believe* my day, I swear! I was out with Dallas and then... and then we—(*She begins laughing uncontrollably.*)

PIPER: You...?

ZOEY: We were talking... (*Still laughing.*)

PIPER: And drinking, by the sounds of it.

ZOEY: Dallas! Me and Dallas...Dallas and I— (*She tries to tell the story but all that comes out is laughter. PIPER and LEAH nod along. They're good at this charade.*)

LEAH: You and Dallas went for drinks?

PIPER: You got day drunk?

ZOEY: And then Dallas...he realizes—

PIPER:	What'd you buy?
ZOEY:	He's like, "WHOA. My sister's baby shower is tonight!" And I'm all "Well you can't show up, there's gonna be *babies* there!"
LEAH:	He did not go to a baby shower drunk.
ZOEY:	Otherwise the baby would get drunk!
PIPER:	I don't think it works that way.
ZOEY:	I know! But that's what I said! And he started laughing so hard he spilt his beer on the server! And *she* got so mad she cut him off!
PIPER:	What'd you buy?
ZOEY:	OH! Well I only bought a few things from wherever, BUT, I stole this jacket from Value Village...(*Searches for the jacket.*)
LEAH:	I thought you were gonna stop stealing things.
ZOEY:	I know, I know, but this bitch also said she'd go vegan with Charlie last month and guess who ate wings with a gorgeous boy today.
PIPER:	Don't you already have a jacket like that?
ZOEY:	I need another one! Because! I'm going to sew stuff on it and bedazzle it and make it my new project. HA! Anyway, what have you gals been up to?
LEAH:	We watched *Pirates*.
ZOEY:	The first one?
PIPER:	Obviously.
ZOEY:	Good. Otherwise I would have thrown my boot at you.

LEAH: Oh come on, the rest of them aren't *that* bad.

               ZOEY throws a boot in LEAH's direction.

PIPER: Okay, you have GOT to stop throwing your shoes around this place.

ZOEY: *(Laughing.)* Don't tempt me! I've still got one more.

LEAH: How 'bout you go to bed, Zo. It's late.

ZOEY: It's only ten! You grannies over there just think it's late because for whatever reason you started your movie at what, six?

PIPER: Seven.

ZOEY: Seven! MY GOD, guys. We gotta go out! Hit up the streets!

PIPER: *(Going to the kitchen.)* You gotta drink some water.

ZOEY: I'm serious! Leah. You wanna go out, don't you?

LEAH: Oh, I don't know...

ZOEY: The night is young! Now come on, you can borrow some of my clothes. Go to my closet, pick whatever you want— just not my new romper—put some lipstick on and let's go!

PIPER: *(Returning with a glass of water.)* We're not going out, Zoey. Drink this.

ZOEY: Why not?

PIPER: Because... we just don't feel like it.

ZOEY: You NEVER feel like it. Come on, guys. Is it so much to ask of my dear dear roommate and my dear dear cousin to come out for a night on the town with yours truly? Seriously, Leah, I haven't seen you in forever! You don't answer my texts anymore, you don't return my calls. You don't even respond to the *memes* I tag you in, like WHAT THE HELL.

LEAH: I've been busy.

LEAH: I'm fine.

ZOEY: Bullshit! You never ignore me. And you look different.

LEAH: I've just lost some weight.

ZOEY: Oh! Well good for you. But for the record, your body is your body and it's not any of my business.

PIPER: How 'bout another movie! Maybe a scary one?

LEAH: I might go home actually.

PIPER: No!

LEAH: *(To Piper.)* I'm just tired. Thanks for having me over.

PIPER: We don't have to watch a scary movie. We could watch a happy one, where everyone is happy and no one yells.

ZOEY: Yeah, stay a while. I'll make us food since we're staying in for the night.

         ZOEY goes to the kitchen. LEAH gathers her stuff.

PIPER: *(Quietly, so that ZOEY doesn't hear.)* You *cannot* leave me here to tell her.

LEAH:	I'm not telling her when she's like this.
ZOEY:	*(Re-entering with the container of cashews soaking in water.)* Okay what the hell is this?
PIPER:	It's gonna be cheese.
ZOEY:	*Cheese?*
PIPER:	It's some vegan thing Charlie's making. You soak the cashews for a day and then blend them.
ZOEY:	That doesn't sound like cheese.
PIPER:	It's not.
LEAH:	All right, I'm heading out.
ZOEY:	Are you avoiding me?
LEAH:	What— no!
ZOEY:	Well it just seems weird that you—
LEAH:	I'm just tired.
PIPER:	Come back tomorrow!
LEAH:	Maybe. Anyway, I gotta go.
ZOEY:	Suit yourself.
LEAH:	Bye, guys!
PIPER:	Bye.
ZOEY:	Acknowledge my memes!

LEAH rushes out. ZOEY eats one of the cashews. She immediately regrets it.

ZOEY:	Oh— ew. No no no.
PIPER:	We have some pizza in the fridge, you know.

ZOEY:	*(She goes to the kitchen.)* So what's up with her?
PIPER:	Leah? She's just having a rough time right now.
ZOEY:	What happened?
PIPER:	It's a long story.
ZOEY:	Well it's not like I'm going anywhere.
PIPER:	Have you checked the group today?
ZOEY:	*(Returning with pizza.)* Did she post in there?
PIPER:	*(Getting her laptop.)* Just read it.
ZOEY:	She never posts anything.
PIPER:	She just wasn't sure how it would go. Thought some people wouldn't believe her.
ZOEY:	Believe her?…wait *what*.
PIPER:	Just read it.
ZOEY:	Was she…?
PIPER:	Just go in the actual group and like—
ZOEY:	Did she get…?
PIPER:	I really think you should just—
ZOEY:	Did someone assault my little cousin?
PIPER:	… just read her post.
ZOEY:	ARE YOU KIDDING ME? / Why didn't she tell me?
PIPER:	Okay, calm down. She was scared to speak up on this one.

ZOEY: Who the hell does she think we are! Of course we'd believe her, that's *kind of* the *point* of this whole group!

PIPER: Don't—don't shoot the messenger!

ZOEY: Yeah, no shit. Who *do* I need to shoot? I swear, if I ever meet the douche bag who assaulted my little Leah, I swear to god—

PIPER: You can't can't lose your shit—freak out like that on this one!

ZOEY: I will march right up to him and I will punch him directly in the face.

PIPER: This one's different.

ZOEY: Does Charlie know?

PIPER: She read the post but she doesn't know the details.

ZOEY: What details?

PIPER: Like, she knows what happened but she doesn't know who did it.

ZOEY: Who did it? (*Piper looks away.*) ...Piper. Who took advantage of my cousin?

PIPER: I mean, I didn't even see this coming. I can't imagine how Charlie's gonna feel.

ZOEY: Answer the question or I will throw my other boot.

PIPER: *Josh*. Josh did it.

          ......And Charlie doesn't know.

          CHARLIE comes home.

ZOEY: Charlie!

PIPER: Hey!

CHARLIE: Zoey!

ZOEY: Talk about timing.

PIPER: Zoey got day-drunk with Dallas today.

CHARLIE: Ooooh with Dallas, huh?

ZOEY: Shut up. Charlie, have you checked the group recently?

CHARLIE: Not since earlier, I was just out with Josh. Also, can you believe that guy bought *another* Vampire Weekend shirt? Like, I told / him not to but—

ZOEY: Yadda yadda whoopee that's great. The group, Charlie. Did you read Leah's post?

CHARLIE: Yeah, we invited her over. When is she coming?

PIPER: She already left.

ZOEY: *For some reason* she wasn't feeling so hot.

CHARLIE: How's she doing?

PIPER: She's holding it together.

ZOEY: The girl looks awful.

CHARLIE: Why'd she leave?

ZOEY: An excellent question! Read the post.

CHARLIE: Yeah I skimmed it earlier. It sounds horrible.

PIPER: Zoey, *you* still have yet to read the post.

ZOEY: I know enough.

CHARLIE: Did Leah make another post or something?

PIPER: No—read the *comments.*

CHARLIE: What happened?

ZOEY: JUST READ THE POST.

CHARLIE: *Okay,* chill.

> *She reads. It sinks in.*

PIPER: It gets worse.

CHARLIE: Haley…Quinta…Paige…

PIPER: Even Gabby.

ZOEY: *Gabby?*

PIPER: Before she moved.

ZOEY: So he's been like this for years?

PIPER: You would know that if you actually *read the post.*

CHARLIE: Wait, guys…are you sure?

ZOEY: You don't believe her?

CHARLIE: No I *do,* just—

PIPER: So what do we do?

CHARLIE: There's no way… they must be mistaken or something.

PIPER: There's no way they're *all* lying.

CHARLIE: I'm not saying they're *lying*—

ZOEY: Then what *are* you saying?

CHARLIE: I don't know. But guys, Josh wouldn't do something like that.

ZOEY: Well he did.

CHARLIE: No, he would have told me—no, he would never have let me—no, no this just doesn't add up, it doesn't make sense.

ZOEY: Doesn't make sense that he would get super close with the founder of a feminist club to make it look like he's on our side and then screw us over?

CHARLIE: Kay, shut up and let me think for a sec.

ZOEY: *(Pulling out her phone.)* Don't worry, I'll call him.

PIPER: You can't.

ZOEY: Sure I can.

PIPER: It's against the rules. We don't do anything without the victim's permission.

ZOEY: Leah won't mind. She'll probably thank me.

CHARLIE: Whoa, whoa, what are you gonna do, kill him?

ZOEY: I don't know, I'm out of boots to throw so it might come down to that.

PIPER: Oh chill out, Zoey. / Charlie, what do you think?

ZOEY: DON'T TELL ME TO CHILL OUT.

PIPER: Well you're being irrational!

ZOEY: I'M FINE.

PIPER: THEN WHY ARE YOU YELLING?

CHARLIE:	*Guys!* We're not doing anything. Not yet.
PIPER:	*(To ZOEY.)* You haven't even read the post.
ZOEY:	If you say that one more time, Piper, *I swear to god.*
PIPER:	Eat me!
CHARLIE:	GUYS calm down.
ZOEY:	I'm not gonna calm down, Charlie. Your best friend raped my little cousin.
CHARLIE:	So let me go talk to him before you do anything! Because—because... well you just said it, he's my best friend... or maybe he's not anymore, I don't know...
ZOEY:	You can't possibly stay friends with him after this...*(Off her look.)* Oh my god.
CHARLIE:	I'm going back to his place.
ZOEY:	Are you kidding me?
PIPER:	Oh leave her alone, Zo. There's more to it than that.
ZOEY:	No no, I'm curious. Charlie! Before you walk out that door, look at me and tell me you believe Leah.
PIPER:	Zoey just—
ZOEY:	No, I'm interested! Charlie. The almighty leader and creator of this secret, sacred group where we all go to be heard and listened to, *do you believe Leah?*
CHARLIE:	Yes.

LEAH continues her post in "Tell Us What Happened."

LEAH: So I went to my first university party. I guess I should mention that I'm only seventeen, I'm a February baby. I pre-drank at my friend's house and then we walked over. I should have known not to drink that much, but I did. Then some guy asked if I wanted to play beer pong with him and for some reason I did. I think I was just caught up in the atmosphere. I've kind of had a thing for this guy in my Drama 111 class, even though he's in his final year of Education—he's a few years older than me. Things start to get pretty foggy for me at this point, but I can remember sitting on the front steps with him towards the middle of the party and then we shared a cigarette and then we kissed and then we ended up at his apartment and that's when I started to get kinda scared.

> *Shift. Early hours of the morning. CHARLIE sits on the floor with a beer reading old journals and newspaper clippings. ZOEY comes home and is startled by CHARLIE.*

ZOEY: *Oh my god!*

CHARLIE: Sorry.

ZOEY: Shit, you scared me. What are you doing?

CHARLIE: Where were you?

ZOEY: I went to see Leah. Why?

CHARLIE: You're home early.

ZOEY: It's almost 2 a.m.

CHARLIE: SHIT really? I thought it was only—

ZOEY: What's all this?

CHARLIE: I'm just thinking.

ZOEY: About what?

CHARLIE: You know what.

ZOEY: I know *what*, I just don't know what there is to think about.

CHARLIE: Yes you do, / don't act like this case is just like all the others because you and I both know this one is different.

ZOEY: No, actually because as far as I'm concerned it would go against everything we stand for to start pussyfooting around where we all know this is gonna go.

CHARLIE: ... How's Leah?

ZOEY: What did Josh say?

CHARLIE: You first.

ZOEY: What did he say?

CHARLIE: Is Leah okay?

ZOEY: Of course not.

CHARLIE: *(Getting up.)* I should call her.

ZOEY: What did Josh say?

CHARLIE: Shhh, Piper's sleeping.

ZOEY: You're digging yourself deeper.

CHARLIE: *I didn't talk to him.* I started walking to his place and threw up halfway there so I came home.

ZOEY: Actually?

CHARLIE: If you'd like proof you can go check the sidewalk on the corner of Richmond and 59th.

ZOEY: ...Well, good. Now that's out of your system we can buckle down and—

CHARLIE: Are you gonna make me say it?

                              PIPER enters from her room in her pyjamas.

PIPER: You guys know what time it is, right?

CHARLIE: / *Yes.*

ZOEY: *Yes.*

PIPER: Okay just making sure...

ZOEY: If you didn't talk to him when you had the chance, then we might as well go ahead and report him like the rulebook says.

PIPER: *(To CHARLIE.)* I told you she'd say this.

ZOEY: What? It's group protocol. When someone is assaulted, the first order of action is to get the victim to a hospital. And since it's too late for that, we jump to the second order of action which is to report the abuser to their school if applicable or to the cops. And may I remind you, Charlie, that you are the one who / wrote the rulebook.

CHARLIE: Wrote the rulebook, I know.

PIPER: I'm sure she didn't have Josh in mind when she wrote it, though.

ZOEY: What, so just because he's Charlie's best friend that means Leah wasn't raped?

PIPER: Our rules don't specify what we're supposed to do with *this* case.

ZOEY: That's only true if you think Josh deserves special treatment.

CHARLIE: Guys, I can handle this.

ZOEY: Says the girl who barfed on her way to go "handle it."

PIPER: *(Looking at the things CHARLIE has been reading on the floor.)* What's all this?

CHARLIE: Nothing.

PIPER: How old is this journal?

CHARLIE: *(Taking it from PIPER.)* High school, doesn't matter.

PIPER: *(Picking up a couple of the newspaper clippings.)* Charlie, seriously, why do you keep all this stuff? "Local Hockey Team Raises Over $6000 for Burn Treatment Centre." Is that *Brandon*?

CHARLIE: From when he made the front page with his hockey team.

PIPER: You've kept this article even after everything he did to you?

CHARLIE: Sometimes I forget that bad people still do good things.

ZOEY: Throw that out. Seriously. That guy was toxic. Him and all his buddies.

CHARLIE: I cut him out of my life years ago. This is just a reminder that the world isn't "fair."

ZOEY: The world not being fair isn't a good enough reason for us brush it off when people hurt people.

CHARLIE: It's also not a good enough reason for us to hurt people in return.

PIPER: Can we please discuss this in the morning?

CHARLIE: She's right. I'm going to bed.

ZOEY: All right, fine. Just one more thing.

                  ZOEY grabs the newspaper clipping from CHARLIE's hand and rips it up.

ZOEY: Good things don't count if a bad person did them.

                  Shift. The next day. PIPER sits on the floor, working on another craft project. LEAH and ZOEY sit on the couch.

ZOEY: So Quinta's dad works for the school and Haley's mom is a lawyer and they talked to them and as long you report it ASAP, the school might be able to do something because he *has* been reported before.

LEAH: Then why hasn't anything been done?

PIPER: Schools have a tendency to—

ZOEY: Reporting guys like this to a university almost never does anything.

LEAH: Then why do people bother?

PIPER: Generally it's in an effort to—

ZOEY: Because if they report someone and nothing happens, at least the next time someone reports that person, they'll have a documented track record. So in this case, Haley and Jenny have already gone to campus administration about him, and nothing happened, so we're hoping that if *you* go—

LEAH: But how do we know they won't just file it like they do with everyone else?

PIPER: Three girls reporting one guy is enough to make a case—we *hope*.

LEAH: But shouldn't it be enough if just one—

ZOEY: Don't get me started on that.

PIPER: It's also worth noting that you're the first girl to come forward about something this serious. All the girls before you have reported stuff that's considered more "lowball." Like, Gabby said he made out with her after a party when she didn't really want to. And Haley said that he—

LEAH: But shouldn't the school take something like that just as seriously as—

ZOEY: Well if you ask any school, they'll say they "take these matters very seriously."

LEAH: But that's just stupid!

ZOEY: Again, / don't get me started.

PIPER: Don't get her started.

ZOEY: What we're saying is, we're all behind you on reporting him. *If* you decide to.

LEAH: Do people ever regret reporting this stuff?

PIPER: Depends on the person, really. It can take a long time. Around a year of scary meetings and pantsuits and reliving the experience and not having enough evidence and trying to hide it from your parents and even if the legal system *does* end up doing something—

ZOEY: Ever heard the term "unfounded"?

LEAH: That doesn't sounds good…

ZOEY:	It means the police see the report as more of an *allegation* of an offence that / "did not occur, nor was it attempted."
PIPER:	"Did not occur, nor was it attempted."
ZOEY:	—and as it so happens, a lot of rape reports go to the dinky little police factory to be processed into some dinky little file labelled *"unfounded."*
LEAH:	Are you serious?
PIPER:	/ Unfortunately.
ZOEY:	YUP. So we're thinking that if you report to the *school*, that's a slightly smaller scale and could actually—
LEAH:	What does Charlie think I should do?
PIPER:	She won't be home till later tonight, so you'll have to wait to talk to her.
ZOEY:	Well you can't talk to her tonight actually because we're going to that show, remember?
PIPER:	I thought that was next week.
ZOEY:	Oh my god I told you like a thousand times it's tonight.
LEAH:	Is Charlie going?
ZOEY:	No, she wants to stay home.
PIPER:	Because Josh is coming over.
ZOEY:	/ Wait *what?*
LEAH:	Wait *what?*

PIPER:	*(Piper hadn't meant to let that slip.)* I just overheard her on the phone with him this morning. She invited him over—presumably to talk about *(Motions to LEAH.)*
ZOEY:	Why wouldn't she tell us that?
PIPER:	Gee, I can't think of a single reason why Charlie wouldn't want us to know that she's inviting Leah's abuser over tonight.
LEAH:	Okay but what if we go through all this trouble and nothing happens?
ZOEY:	Leah, you're still seventeen. Josh is twenty-two.
LEAH:	So?
PIPER:	You're still a minor. I mean, technically you're over the age of consent, but you're still below the age of majority.
ZOEY:	And *that's* what I call "a window of opportunity."
LEAH:	Okay?
PIPER:	It means it's bad—worse than the other cases. It means—
ZOEY:	It means we could *win* for once! *(The room stops.)*…we could win this. We just need your consent.

Shift. LEAH continues reciting her post.

LEAH:	I kind of remember stumbling into his place, but I was pretty done by that point. Like, I liked this guy and everything but all I wanted to do was go back to the party and find my friends. I just didn't know how to say that, or like, "I dunno I just didn't say anything I guess.

PIPER makes a post in the group.

PIPER   Content Warning: Boys are stupid.

So this guy dumped me 53 days ago and for a while I thought I was doing a lot better but I think I'm starting to get bad again. I know he's toxic and everything but I still feel so empty and I'm trying to get my shit together but I just can't. I don't know why I'm like this.

Shift. Evening. JOSH enters The Clubhouse.

JOSH: Yo!

CHARLIE: *(Entering from her room with her laptop.)* Hey.

JOSH: So Julia loved her gift. She's been looking for cool pins to put on her backpack, so props to you 'cause I never would've thought to get her *pins* of all things.

CHARLIE: Oh good.

JOSH: Yeah.

Silence. CHARLIE looks at JOSH. He looks back, confused.

JOSH: So what happened the other night after we were out shopping? When you texted me that you were on your way over?

CHARLIE: I got halfway to your place then chickened out.

JOSH: What, why? ...You okay?

CHARLIE: You never told me you were going to the Zeta Psi party.

JOSH: Which one?

CHARLIE:	The "welcome back" party. In September. I was gonna go, but I didn't want to go alone so I asked if you were going and you said you weren't.
JOSH:	Well, I ended up going with Ethan and Tommy. But I think I left pretty early.
CHARLIE:	Do you know Gabby Carlson?
JOSH:	Who?
CHARLIE:	Gabby Carlson. She goes to UBC now.
JOSH:	Then why would I know her?
CHARLIE:	You tell me.
JOSH:	What's going on?
CHARLIE:	Why didn't you tell me you were going to that party?
JOSH:	I thought we were talking about Gabby what's-her-face.
CHARLIE:	I'm changing my mind. Girls do that.
JOSH:	Was Gabby at that party or something?
CHARLIE:	When was the last time Leah Madison showed up to your Drama class?
JOSH:	Now *this*? I don't know.
CHARLIE:	Well *think*.
JOSH:	I don't know! A while ago.
CHARLIE:	You know Gabby Carlson from high school. You two met at the football tournament and you took her out for lunch a couple times and then—

JOSH: Why are you saying this like you were there? / You weren't there.

CHARLIE: And then you convinced her to leave the last party early with you and go back to your place and then when you guys got to your house you made out—

JOSH: Okay, okay. So maybe I do remember her now that you say all that. We just made out a little. How do you know about that?

CHARLIE: She told me.

JOSH: You guys still talk?

CHARLIE: No, she told me three years ago. But I had no idea she was talking about you.

JOSH: Okay...Cool?

CHARLIE: I would have gone to that party if you had told me you were going.

JOSH: Well like I said, I went with Ethan and Tommy and I know you don't like Ethan so I didn't bother inviting you.

CHARLIE: How much did you drink that night.

JOSH: I don't know, a few beers?

CHARLIE: No like, what specifically / I really need to know.

JOSH: Kay, why are you interrogating me like this?

CHARLIE: Just tell me what you drank!

JOSH: I don't remember *exactly*, okay? I didn't blackout or anything, though.

CHARLIE: You weren't blackout.

JOSH: *No.* Not that it's any of your business. But no, I wasn't blackout…Are you gonna tell me what's going on?

CHARLIE: I will. Just tell me what happened first.

JOSH: Okay…I pre-drank with the guys, we walked over, there were a ton of people there—as usual—and it was pretty wild—as usual— and there were a couple kegs—as usual—and me and that girl from my Drama class played Ethan and Katie in beer pong, and they lost— as usual—and then we ended up hanging out and stuff after that. Happy?

CHARLIE: "Hanging out and stuff"?...What the fuck does that mean?

JOSH: Kay, whoa, what's wrong with you?

CHARLIE: I'm fine.

JOSH: Everything okay?

CHARLIE: No, but before I tell you I just—…Did you and Leah have sex that night? I know that's a blunt question, but—

JOSH: I mean, kinda yeah.

CHARLIE: "Yeah" as in…?

JOSH: As in yeah, we went back to my place and fooled around for a bit. Satisfied?

CHARLIE: And you remember all of it.

JOSH: I mean, yeah. Like, I was drunk—we *both* were—but like, it was fine. Probably pretty sloppy, I don't know. Can we stop talking about this now?

CHARLIE: What, 'cause we've never talked about our sex lives before?

JOSH:	There's a difference between talking about it for fun and being *interrogated*.
CHARLIE:	What about Paige Danforth, do you remember her?
JOSH:	Charlie—
CHARLIE:	And Quinta Ryan?
JOSH:	Oh my god…
CHARLIE:	Do you remember them?
JOSH:	Don't change the subject.
CHARLIE:	I know you do.
JOSH:	So why are you asking?
CHARLIE:	I'm not the one changing the subject.
JOSH:	You're freaking me out.
CHARLIE:	So are you.
JOSH:	*Why?*
CHARLIE:	Because I didn't know they were talking about you!
JOSH:	Who? Those girls?
CHARLIE:	Yeah!
JOSH:	What, Gabby Carlson told you all about me *in high school?*
CHARLIE:	Yeah.
JOSH:	Don't give me that, you two weren't friends.
CHARLIE:	I mean, we kinda were. Behind the scenes.
JOSH:	*What is that supposed to mean?*

CHARLIE:	Whoa, kay, why are you yelling at me?
JOSH:	*I'm not*—I wasn't yelling. I'm just…how did they tell you this stuff? Are you like, spying on me or something?
CHARLIE:	No, I'm not spying on you. They *told* me. Gabby told me four years ago, and Paige and Quinta told me a couple years back, and Leah—
JOSH:	Okay…so you know a lot of details about my personal life. Great.
CHARLIE:	It's more complicated than that. Do you remember like, asking them…?
JOSH:	What, like, for consent and stuff?
CHARLIE:	Yes. For "consent and stuff."
JOSH:	I mean…yeah?
CHARLIE:	Josh…
JOSH:	Well, what do you want from me? How well do you remember sexual encounters from *four years ago*?
CHARLIE:	Leah wasn't that long ago. Did you ask her?
JOSH:	Yeah…yeah! I did. I asked. She was kinda drunk, I was kinda drunk, we messed around, I *asked*, she agreed and that was it.
CHARLIE:	Leah was *really* drunk.
JOSH:	Yeah, that's what I said.
CHARLIE:	You said she was *kinda* drunk. I'm saying she was *really* drunk. There's a difference, / you should know that!
JOSH:	I know there's a difference!

CHARLIE: KAY. When was the last time Leah showed up to your Drama class?

JOSH: Not since like...wait.

CHARLIE: Josh, I'm trying really hard to—

JOSH: Why hasn't she been showing up to class?

CHARLIE: People are starting to talk and I am doing everything I can to—

JOSH: Are you trying to tell me that I—

CHARLIE: I don't want anything bad to happen to you because you're my best friend and you have been my best friend ever since high school but—

JOSH: What are people saying?

CHARLIE: And if it were *just* Leah, it would be different, but it's not just Leah, it's Gabby and Haley and Paige / and Jenny and Quinta.

JOSH: Whoa whoa whoa, I didn't have sex with all those girls.

CHARLIE: But you still crossed a line with them.

JOSH: HOW DO YOU KNOW ALL THIS.

CHARLIE: THEY TOLD ME.

JOSH: / How? When?

CHARLIE: Gabby said "no"! She agreed to go back to your place but she never wanted to make out with you. And Haley and Anika both said the same thing, that you didn't really listen to them and got too close and Paige said that she didn't want to but didn't know how to say no and then—

JOSH: So what are you saying?

CHARLIE: I'm saying you really need to get your fucking
                story straight.

JOSH: Well what is the big deal about Leah? It
                happened, there was alcohol involved, it
                maybe wasn't the most formal event, but like,
                drunk sex happens! You know? Shit happens.
                And like...I don't know, we can both just
                agree to forget about it if that's what she
                wants. I haven't told anyone.

CHARLIE: She actually can't forget it.

JOSH: I didn't assault her. (Nothing from CHARLIE.)
                Charlie, would I rape someone?

CHARLIE: … it's just that all these girls are saying—

JOSH: So what, it's their word over mine!

CHARLIE: Kay I really need you to understand that I'm
                trying to help you here. There's talk of getting
                you suspended! Or maybe even expelled.

JOSH: Who's gonna get me expelled?

CHARLIE: I've never told you about the group I run. But
                I started this like, network of girls and Piper
                and Zoey and I run the group and—

JOSH: What does this have to do with me getting
                expelled in my final year?

CHARLIE: For the past three years, I've been running an online group called "Tell Us What Happened" and people can go and connect with each other about shit like this. And right now, a bunch of people in that group are realizing that they've all been hurt by the same guy and that guy happens to be you. And Zoey— because Leah's like her little cousin who she protects like crazy—heard about what happened between you and Leah and now she's—

JOSH: Well you have to stop them.

CHARLIE: I can't do that.

JOSH: So you're gonna get me expelled?

CHARLIE: I'm not sure what I'm gonna do.

JOSH: Well figure it out! Shut it down! Look, I can't get expelled. I'm almost done! I'm gonna be a *teacher*. I'm gonna be a role model for all those kids. I'm a good guy, Charlie. Come on, you know that!

CHARLIE: I don't know what I know anymore.

JOSH: Dude—look at me—you *know* me. I wouldn't ever intentionally harm somebody, *especially* a girl.

CHARLIE: But what if you didn't realize you were hurting them?

JOSH: Well what if Leah said "yes"? What if she wanted to and just regrets it because she's never hooked up with someone she doesn't know that well?

CHARLIE: She wouldn't make this up.

JOSH:

Regardless, I'm gonna go ahead and say that being publicly accused of rape ruins your life more than getting raped does!

That one stings. He can tell.

Shift. ZOEY makes a post in "Tell Us What Happened."

ZOEY:

Content warning. Cigarettes.

I just wanted to make a little celebratory post in here that I have officially gone an entire month without a cigarette. I know it doesn't sound like much but the guy I'm seeing right now is a huge social smoker so it's been really tough to resist but I did it! Anyway. Looking forward to seeing you all soon at the anniversary party!

CHARLIE makes a post.

CHARLIE:

Hey lovelies. I just wanted to pop in and say that I know I haven't been responding to a lot of your messages lately and I wanted to apologize. I'm trying to deal with life and run this group at the same time and it's getting to be a real struggle. Just know that I love all of you and I'm trying my best.

Shift. Night. PIPER has made a mess. Hard rock music is blasting. She stands on the couch in the living room, cutting up her artwork and letting the pieces fall into a metal garbage can. CHARLIE enters through the front door, coming home from work.

CHARLIE:

What are you doing? ....Piper! *(She unplugs the music.)*

PIPER:

I was listening to that.

CHARLIE: What is going on?

PIPER: I'm chopping up my art, what does it look like? Turn it back on.

CHARLIE: What happened?

PIPER: Turn it back on!

CHARLIE: Not until you tell me what's going on.

PIPER: I'm fine. NOTHING'S HAPPENING.

CHARLIE: Piper, look at me.

PIPER: You know, it's crazy how much fucking artwork we accumulate in this fucking house I fucking swear to god.

CHARLIE: Is Zoey home?

PIPER: She's out with Dallas. Like, I didn't think I'd get through all of it, but here I am, an hour later, and I'm almost out of stuff to slice before I burn it all.

CHARLIE: You're not gonna burn it.

PIPER: Fuck you, yeah I am!

CHARLIE: Piper, I need you to look at me.

PIPER: THEN I thought, "I know! I'll burn the manifesto!"

CHARLIE: No!

PIPER: (*Holds up a highly decorated, three-year-old, cherished work of art.*) I dug it up!

CHARLIE: Did you sleep last night?

PIPER: Turn the music back on, this isn't as fun without it.

CHARLIE: Did you go outside today?

PIPER: IT'S TOO QUIET WE NEED TO MAKE SOME NOISE IN THIS PLACE!

CHARLIE: *(Grabbing the scissors and the stack of artwork.)* Sit.

PIPER: Give it BACK!

CHARLIE: *Look at me.*

PIPER looks at her, nearly shaking.

CHARLIE: We're just in the living room, okay? It's just you and me in the living room.

PIPER: I need it.

CHARLIE: *(Handing over the papers.)* I'm keeping the scissors. Now are you gonna tell me what happened?

PIPER: I don't wanna try anymore.

CHARLIE: You don't wanna try with…art anymore, or—…?

PIPER: All of it. Art, boys, girls, love, life, I'm just done.

CHARLIE: Did you go outside today?

PIPER: Just out for tea.

CHARLIE: Where?

PIPER: Doesn't matter.

CHARLIE: You went to Safe Leaf, didn't you?

PIPER: No!

CHARLIE: Andre was working, wasn't he?

PIPER: I didn't even make it there. I walked past his apartment and turned around.

CHARLIE: Why?

PIPER: It doesn't even matter! I don't care what anybody thinks.

CHARLIE: Did you see him, did he say something?

PIPER: I just saw that he'd put it all outside. So I took it all home.

CHARLIE: Took what home?

PIPER: It was all just on the ground outside his building. Everything I'd ever made for him, all my paintings and drawings and bullshit. And they had been there for a while because they were all rained on. Some of them had bird shit on them.

CHARLIE: Oh, I'm so sorry.

PIPER: Don't be. I needed to see it.

CHARLIE: And you were hoping to chat with him at Safe Leaf.

PIPER: No.

CHARLIE: Come on, I know you're wearing blue lipstick because it's his favourite. You've got to move on. I know it sucks but you're not alone. You are valid and worthy—

PIPER: Well, I'm done with those stupid mantras, it's all bullshit. I mean, we're kidding ourselves if we think we're gonna make any difference.

CHARLIE: I know it feels that way sometimes but you've gotta remember that you've got a whole team of warriors on your side.

PIPER: "Warriors"? When are you gonna wake up and see this group for what we really are? A bunch of sad loser girls who hide behind screens and complain about their feelings.

CHARLIE: It's more than that and you know it. / Look, I know you're mad right now—

PIPER: IT'S NOT MORE THAN THAT. It's not it's not / it's not it's not it's not it's—

CHARLIE: Piper, I need you to look at me and take a deep breath, okay—

PIPER: It's not anything more than a stupid Facebook group! We just type our problems into a screen so that a bunch of girls we hardly know can comment a bunch of heart emojis!

CHARLIE: You don't mean that.

PIPER: At least I'm doing something about my problem. Sitting around drawing all day isn't getting me anywhere, so I'm gonna burn it and get a fresh start.

CHARLIE: Let's smoke or something.

PIPER: I'm gonna burn this first. Where's my lighter?

CHARLIE: Just do one thing for me, before you burn it? Read the manifesto. Out loud.

PIPER: ...I don't even care about the group anymore.

CHARLIE: Then you won't mind reading it.

PIPER: ... fine...but I'm still gonna burn it.

"This is a safe space for anybody who has been made to feel ashamed of themselves. This is a group to share stories about any struggles you are experiencing while trying to navigate this patriarchal society, or just this thing called LIFE. This group is here because the world is trying to tear us apart. Because the media tells us we are 'less than.' Because right now a girl is being abused and doesn't know how much longer she can hold on. Because she might not even know it's abuse. Because she's being told it's her fault. Because you might know that girl. Because you might *be* that girl. We need to stand together as girls and we need to realize that when one of us gets hurt, we all get hurt. Standing by has been normalized. Acceptance has been internalized. It is not enough to 'reclaim' the tropes, we must rewrite the entire mythology. It is up to us to change the system, and we will change it together as one powerful female unit. Because together, WE ARE THE REVOLUTION."

PIPER puts the manifesto down on the table.

PIPER: Sorry I spilled Red Bull on it.

PIPER leaves with the trash can. CHARLIE picks up the manifesto and begins to read it again.

LEAH continues her post in the group.

LEAH: I wish I could remember more but next thing I knew we were in his room and my clothes were off and we were having sex. And I remember telling him I had just lost my virginity a couple months ago and I can remember being like "I haven't had a lot of sex" and he just kept telling me "It's okay, it's okay. Don't worry." And afterwards he fell asleep, so I just Ubered home.

Shift. ZOEY sitting in the living room working on her laptop. PIPER enters with some magazines and begins to cut things out, working on another project.

ZOEY: You're coming to campus with us on Monday, right?

PIPER: Oh, uhm. I don't think so.

ZOEY: If Charlie were going, would you go?

PIPER: I don't know, maybe.

ZOEY: Whose side are you on?

PIPER: It's not Charlie's fault she has a midterm and can't go.

ZOEY: So you're on her side?

PIPER: There aren't sides. I'm in the middle.

ZOEY: If you're in the middle, you're admitting there are sides.

PIPER: That's not what I meant.

ZOEY: You know what, forget it. Just go crying to Charlie when she gets back and stay home all day on Monday, what do I care?

PIPER: You're just mad because you're not the leader.

ZOEY: I'm not mad at anybody, I'm just disappointed that you've become such a flake.

PIPER: When did you start hating me?

ZOEY: I don't hate you. Don't you see? I care about you so damn much and every day I have to sit here and watch you sit around being a flake.

PIPER: I'm not a flake.

ZOEY: You are. And I'm sorry to be the one to tell you that, but someone has to. Sitting around at home all the time whenever you're not working at the bookstore, and waiting for Charlie's permission to do anything—

PIPER: I do stuff!

ZOEY: No, you don't. But you said you would. We all said we would when we wrote the Tell Us What Happened Manifesto together.

PIPER: You're not the one who created that group, you know.

ZOEY: Well, I seem to be the only one who cares about Leah.

PIPER: Fine! Fine, you wanna know what I want? I'll go with you and Leah to report him on Monday.

ZOEY: But don't do that because it's what I want, do it because it's what—

PIPER: I want you to shut up.

> *Neither is sure what comes next. CHARLIE comes home from work. PIPER scurries to her room.*

CHARLIE: Hey, were you two just fighting?

ZOEY: Nope...Leah's on her way over.

CHARLIE: Oh, nice...How was your day?

ZOEY: It was good...I bought a fish.

CHARLIE: Really? Where it is, what kind?

ZOEY: It's at Dallas's place. We bought it together. A beta fish.

CHARLIE: Oooooooh, you guys are getting serious, hey?

ZOEY: It's just a fish.

CHARLIE: Are you sure about that?

ZOEY: It's just a fish. We named him Larry.

> *CHARLIE gets a bag of chips from the kitchen to snack on. ZOEY watches, waiting for her to say it.*

ZOEY: So...?

CHARLIE: It's complicated.

ZOEY: Classic.

CHARLIE: He was drunk and so was Leah.

ZOEY: So then we go off what the survivor says.

CHARLIE: If we're gonna take serious action on this I'd like to be 100% sure we're in the right. Plus, I didn't create this group to make a bunch of vigilante justice girls.

ZOEY: Oh is *that* what we're doing?

CHARLIE: You're about to tear Josh apart, you know.

ZOEY: Which is another way of saying that I'm doing your job.

CHARLIE: My job is to provide a safe space where—

ZOEY: I know the rules! Now do me a favour and think back to when you were seventeen and started the group. And remember how lonely and scared and sad you were. That's where Leah is right now. And the only reason you survived that year was because you had a group of girls behind you.

CHARLIE: I also had Josh. And anyway, Leah's stronger than I was.

ZOEY: Leah looks up to you more than anyone. Even more than me.

CHARLIE: That's not true.

ZOEY: Well, you're the girl who got through it, right? You were the fifteen-year-old who got involved with an older guy for two years who took advantage of you—

CHARLIE: I don't need the reminder—

ZOEY: He wrecked your relationship with your parents, your reputation at school—

CHARLIE: My reputation at school was already a shit show.

ZOEY: And you're the girl who was labelled the "School Slut" and forced to—

CHARLIE: *What's your point?*

ZOEY: You're the girl who endured all the bullshit and came out alive—

CHARLIE: You're forgetting everything I lost in the process and how hard it was to start over after that!

ZOEY: THE POINT IS you've been through it all. So when people like Leah come to this group and ask for advice, they may be posing the question to hundreds of people but they're really only asking you. Because they all want to be you.

CHARLIE: Leah would be fine to do this without me, she's seventeen and he's already been reported twice so—

ZOEY: She won't do it until you tell her to.

    She won't listen to me. So do me a favour and before you tell her to keep quiet about all this, think about what seventeen-year-old Charlie would have done if she had the chance to report the boy who made her life a living nightmare.

    LEAH enters the Clubhouse.

LEAH: Hey guys, I was just—...What's going on?

ZOEY: We were just talking about *Joshy*.

LEAH: Charlie, I wanted to ask you about that because I know it would be tough for you to go with us to report him but I just wanted to see—

ZOEY: No, it's fine. Tell her, Charlie. Tell her what you think she should do.

LEAH: It's fine if you don't want me to, I just—

CHARLIE: Just watch what you wear. When you go report him. Make sure your neckline isn't too low and don't wear a lot of makeup and make sure your jeans aren't ripped.

LEAH: Wait, so you're saying—

CHARLIE: *(Going to her room.)* Just trust me. It matters.

> *LEAH continues her post. Throughout the following posts, we see CHARLIE holding the manifesto that PIPER dug up, reading it over and over again.*

LEAH   I think I started crying in the Uber on the way home and I didn't know what to do. I went into my bathroom and looked at myself in the mirror and I was like, "What just happened?" And then I threw up a whole bunch and I ended up passing out on my bathroom floor. I woke up with vomit in my hair.

> *PIPER is making a post.*

PIPER: Content Warning: Relapsing and generally being a disaster.

            I'm sick of being like this. I wanna change but I don't know how. I'm trying to eat but I'm just never hungry and I really miss my ex because he was the only one who could ever help me when I was like this and I just don't know what to do.

> *LEAH continues her post.*

LEAH: I *think* that was rape, but I don't know. I mean, maybe at some point, I gave in and said it was all cool? Honestly, I kind of think it was my fault.

Shift. Late. The sound of a car screeching away. We hear ZOEY fumbling with her keys outside the front door, trying to open it but the key just won't turn. Finally she enters, closes the door behind her and paces the room a bit, replaying his words in her head, checking her phone.

She goes back to the door, opens it, peeks outside, hoping he's maybe outside for some reason. Her heart sinks a bit.

She closes the door, leans against it, and slides down to the floor. She removes her shoes and chucks them at the floor. She gives in and calls him. He doesn't pick up. She leaves a message.

ZOEY: Hey, asshole. You cut me off back there before I could even fucking finish, so I just wanted you to know that *I don't need you either* and I'll be stopping by tomorrow to pick up the fish because if you think you're keeping Larry, you are sorely mistaken.

She hangs up with vengeance. She chucks her phone at the floor. Regretting it, she crosses to her phone and finds a cracked screen.

ZOEY: Dammit.

Shift. Afternoon. PIPER is home alone working on a somewhat tall structure in the middle of the room. A knock at the door. She freezes. She crawls to the window and peeks through the blinds.

PIPER: *Shit.*

Another knock. PIPER decides to hide instead of answering it. She changes her mind. She can do this! She goes to answer it. She chickens out. She'd rather paint than deal with this. Another knock. Quickly, as if ripping off a band-aid, she answers the door. JOSH stands there.

PIPER: Hey, Charlie's not home, you could try coming back later.

JOSH: Your doorbell's broken.

PIPER: It's been like that for over a year. Charlie's not home. You'll have to come back later.

JOSH: Weird, I've never noticed that before. I guess I always just walk in, hey?

PIPER: So I've heard.

A small moment.

PIPER: Charlie's not home right now so—

JOSH: Mind if I wait here for her?

PIPER has not rehearsed an answer for this. It shows.

She's at school, right? She's done at eleven on Fridays and she doesn't usually work till four.

PIPER: Yeah.

JOSH: So...?

PIPER: *(Giving in.)* Sure. Come in. Wait for her. Then go.

He walks in and takes in her project. PIPER stays by the door, staring at him.

JOSH: You gonna close the door, or…?

PIPER: Oh. Right.

JOSH: Working on another project here, hey? Another mythical creature or…?

PIPER: No, this one's more of a conceptual piece.

JOSH: Nice.

PIPER: See, I've already built the basic structure. And now I have to paint it.

JOSH: Nice, nice…

           JOSH checks his phone for the time. PIPER peeks out the window.

PIPER: She's knows you're here, right?

JOSH: Who, Charlie? Oh yeah, we made plans to meet and stuff.

PIPER: Okay, good. Just 'cause I'd probably be in shit if she got home and you were—

JOSH: Yeah, no. Makes sense.

PIPER: Zoey definitely won't be coming home though.

JOSH: Thank god.

PIPER: Yeah, she'd probably shoot you.

JOSH: Wait what?

PIPER: I was kidding.

JOSH: Right, yeah, ha ha…

           For what it's worth, I think your project's gonna be freakin' awesome.

PIPER: I don't know about that, but thanks.

JOSH: No, for real. From what I've seen, you've got real talent.

PIPER: It's just a hobby.

JOSH: Really? 'Cause I'm pretty sure Charlie told me you got into some pretty high-end art school.

PIPER: Charlie has a nasty habit of speaking very highly of the people she cares about.

JOSH: I heard your portfolio was unreal.

PIPER: Well, that's neither here nor there.

JOSH: Did you turn it down? Get rejected?

PIPER: Yeah.

JOSH: You got rejected?

PIPER: No—I turned it down. It's a four-year program. In Montreal.

JOSH: I get it, moving's a lot of money.

PIPER: Not just that…It's a lot to commit to.

JOSH: But if that's the dream—

PIPER: Dreams are overrated.

JOSH: But if that's what you want, you go for it!

PIPER: Gee, thanks, Dad.

JOSH: You could do it, you know.

PIPER: You don't know what I can and can't do.

JOSH: I feel like *you* don't know what you can and can't do.

PIPER:	Well for your information, it's not that simple.
JOSH:	But if it's the dream, then you should—
PIPER:	*It's not that simple!*
JOSH:	… yeah. Yeah no, I get it.
PIPER:	It's just that art school is a ton of work and a ton of money and me and commitment don't have a great history together.
JOSH:	I think you could do it.
PIPER:	I can't even go out for tea without running home crying.
JOSH:	Well you're the only person I know who's *always* working on their craft. For real! I can't think of a time that I've come over and seen you doing something other than finishing your latest project.
PIPER:	Well, that's just convenient timing.
JOSH:	I don't know, man. I'm here a lot.
PIPER:	Not recently.
JOSH:	Well *in the past.* And, hey, if you decide to pursue it in post-secondary, or in life as a career, or *whatever*, I would be rooting for you. Hell, I already am.
PIPER:	Thanks.
	PIPER has never accepted a compliment like that.
PIPER:	Charlie doesn't know you're here, does she? She's gonna be home any minute and I don't want to stir the pot, so…
JOSH:	You want me to leave.

PIPER: If Charlie and Zoey find out I let you in, it's gonna create a big debacle and—

JOSH: Why do you put up with her?

PIPER: Charlie's my best friend.

JOSH: No, Zoey. She walks all over you.

PIPER: She just gets worked up about stuff.

JOSH: So why do you put up with her?

PIPER: It may not appear that way, but Zoey is one of my closest friends. And friends are allowed to go through rough patches.

JOSH: That doesn't mean she can use you as a verbal punching bag.

PIPER: Kay, you came over here to see Charlie and I'm doing you a favour by letting you wait for her, so if your plan is to just pass the time by pointing out all the flaws in my life, I'm gonna need you to kindly get the hell out of here.

JOSH: *(Heading for the door.)* ...sorry.

PIPER: Can't you just message her?

JOSH: She won't respond.

PIPER: Well she did tell you to leave her alone for a while.

JOSH: But that's the thing, how long is "a while"?

PIPER: I don't know, *a while*. A prolonged amount of time. An interval of space. A significant duration between point A and point B.

JOSH: Oh my god...

PIPER:	You asked for a definition of "a while" I'm just trying to help you out.
JOSH:	You know, for someone so shy—
PIPER:	I'm only bugging you because—
JOSH:	I know why you're bugging me!
PIPER:	It's just hard because you're the guy who—
JOSH:	Well if you didn't want to talk to me, why did you let me in?
PIPER:	I felt bad, I panicked!
JOSH:	Well if you want me to go, I'll go!
PIPER:	It's just hard when everyone's always—
JOSH:	*Am I losing Charlie?*
	A moment. Less awkward.
PIPER:	No…I don't know. Maybe.
JOSH:	Piper, I can't lose her. She's the best friend I've ever had.
PIPER:	Look, I can't speak for Charlie, but she's a mess right now.
JOSH:	I'm screwed without her. She's the one who always helps me, you know.
PIPER:	I know. She helps everybody.
JOSH:	And and and, I think this is spreading fast because Julia broke it off with me and and like, I start my last practicum next semester and like, I can't do that and deal with a potential court case and lose Charlie all at the same time.

PIPER: You might have to.

JOSH: But you said it yourself, friends are allowed to go through rough patches, right? Charlie and I—we'll stay friends.

PIPER: ...I think you should go.

JOSH: Right. (*Starting for the door.*) Thanks.

PIPER: For what?

JOSH: For hearing me out. No one else will.

PIPER: Sorry Charlie's not home yet. I don't know what's taking her so long.

JOSH: Well, she's not done class till two.

PIPER: Wait...what?

JOSH: (*Off her look.*) Good luck with your project. I'm sure it'll turn out great.

                JOSH leaves. PIPER closes the door behind him. She leans against the door.

                LEAH continues her post in the group.

LEAH: He just seemed so nice. But still, I could've not drank so much. I could've not played beer pong with him. I could've not shared a cigarette with him. But I did. I should maybe just drop that Drama course. Or maybe all my courses. Sorry for the long post.

                Early evening. LEAH, PIPER and ZOEY are in the living room. ZOEY is pacing.

ZOEY: It's bullshit! This whole system. It's stupid, it's fake—

PIPER: The system isn't broken, it's doing exactly what it was designed to do—

LEAH: That office lady was so mean. Like, so robotic, was she even listening to me?

PIPER: She looked half asleep the whole time.

LEAH: I thought my own *school* would take my side.

ZOEY: The whole thing's flawed—we can't believe the victim and believe that people are innocent until proven guilty at the same time.

LEAH: Does administration think we're *all* lying?

PIPER: Just goes to show how much they actually care about their students.

LEAH: Like, Josh is only one guy. How many others have been reported before?

ZOEY: TOO MANY.

PIPER: VOLUME.

LEAH: *Guys!*

ZOEY: We have to do something.

PIPER: We just did something and it didn't work.

ZOEY: Campus is just one option. There's gotta be something else we can do.

LEAH: I really don't wanna go to the police, though.

PIPER: We could go public with it. Look how fast The Tightrope shut down when that one girl made a Facebook status.

ZOEY: No, guys, there's gotta be a solution to this that doesn't involve social media. We want more than a *trending hashtag* from this.

PIPER: What *do* we want?

LEAH: I want to never see him again. And I want to be the last girl he ever does this to.

PIPER: Oh, I doubt he'll ever do this again. He's really cut up about it.

ZOEY: How do *you* know?

PIPER: He told me.

ZOEY: Whoa whoa whoa—

LEAH: You've talked to him?

PIPER: He came by the house—

ZOEY: And *you let him in*?

PIPER: Kay, I know it was stupid of me but I panicked and I let him in and we talked for like two seconds then I booted him out.

ZOEY: Why didn't you tell us?

PIPER: The point is, he kind of broke down and told me that he can't bear losing Charlie and doing his practicum and dealing with what could maybe turn into a court case all at the same time.

ZOEY: (*Deadpan, miming a violin.*) Here's my violin, I'm so sad for Josh.

LEAH: Didn't he kind of bring all that on himself?

ZOEY: Poor little Josh has to do his practicum with the newfound knowledge that he's a predator.

PIPER: (*An idea.*) Whoa, wait a sec. He's gonna start his practicum.

ZOEY: Yeah, we know.

PIPER: He's gonna be working with teenagers.

LEAH: And that's what gets me, 'cause like, I'm only seventeen and that didn't stop him.

ZOEY: Wait, Piper. Where are you going with this?

PIPER: Well, if Leah said she doesn't want him to do anything like this ever again—

ZOEY: Are you saying we—

PIPER: He'll be spending every day in a room full of seventeen-year-old girls like Leah.

LEAH: So what, are you saying we go warn the high school about him?

PIPER: Just because universities don't prioritize their students' safety doesn't mean that high schools operate the same way.

LEAH: Whoa...

ZOEY: We gotta do it.

LEAH: What if the high school doesn't believe us?

PIPER: That's a top story, right there. "Local High School Knowingly Admits Student Teacher with Sexual Assault Record." At which point, parents get involved.

LEAH: Holy shit.

ZOEY: We're doing it.

PIPER: But still, we would need to figure out which school he's teaching at.

ZOEY: Charlie would know.

LEAH: Think she'd spill?

PIPER:	If we go about it properly.
ZOEY:	Which we will.
PIPER:	Guys, she's home.
LEAH:	Oh my god.
ZOEY:	Kay, chill, it's fine.
LEAH:	I know, I'm just nervous.

CHARLIE comes home.

ZOEY:	/ Hey!
LEAH:	/ Charlie!
PIPER:	You're home!
CHARLIE:	*(Registering their excitement.)* Yeah, we're all here, aren't we?
PIPER:	How was work? Or school? Or both?
CHARLIE:	Work was good. / A little slow but I made—
ZOEY:	Yadda yadda whoopee that's great. So you heard what happened with campus?
CHARLIE:	Yeah, Leah texted me. I can't believe they didn't do anything. I'm so sorry, I swear I thought they would.
LEAH:	So did we.
CHARLIE:	You gotta keep pushing, though.
LEAH:	But what about you and Josh?
CHARLIE:	Doesn't matter.
LEAH:	Are you sure?

CHARLIE: Yes, I'm sure! Guys, I'm done being wishy-washy about this. "We need to stand together as girls," right? And as for Josh...— it's like ripping off a band-aid, I guess.

ZOEY: That's great because speaking of that monster—

PIPER: He stopped by the other day.

CHARLIE: Wait, what?

PIPER: / He stopped by in an attempt to see you the other day while I was—

LEAH: / Piper talked to him a few days ago and apparently he started—

ZOEY: That dickwad came by yesterday and Piper let him inside—

CHARLIE: WHOA. ONE PERSON, PLEASE.

PIPER: / He stopped by hoping to—

ZOEY: That asshole came by—

CHARLIE: FOR THE LOVE OF GOD. Piper. Talk.

PIPER: Josh came to see you on Friday and I didn't know what to do so I let him in and we got to talking and—

CHARLIE: Did he want you to tell me this?

PIPER: No— no, it's just that it got us talking just now about how like, 'cause he's gonna be a teacher, right?

CHARLIE: Yeah.

PIPER: A high school teacher. With *teenagers*. Okay, think about it. Leah is how old?

ZOEY: *Get to the point, Piper.*

PIPER: Okay okay! We were thinking that if it would
                  be okay with you—because Leah said she's
                  okay with it (and we figured we should check
                  with her first)—

ZOEY: MY GOD. Charlie. We need you to tell us
                  which school Josh is gonna be student-
                  teaching at so that we can go tell them he's a
                  sex offender.

LEAH: You wouldn't have to do anything but tell us
                  which school.

PIPER: Which would prevent him from doing his
                  practicum.

LEAH: Would he even be able to graduate without
                  having done a practicum?

PIPER: I doubt it.

ZOEY: *(To CHARLIE.)* So what do you say? It was
                  Piper's idea. Genius! Total genius!

CHARLIE: The problem is that Josh didn't actually tell
                  me where he's student-teaching.

                  The room sinks.

LEAH: Well, there goes that.

ZOEY: He never told you?

CHARLIE: He probably knows by now. But I obviously
                  haven't spoken with him.

ZOEY: Could you find out?

CHARLIE: And say what, "Hey can you give me the
                  name of your practicum school so I can take
                  away your future"?

ZOEY:	Well, don't put it *that* way.
CHARLIE:	I doubt he'd even wanna talk to me right now.
PIPER:	That's *all* he wants, actually. He's worried he's losing you. He'd jump at the chance to hang out like normal.

All eyes on CHARLIE.

PIPER:	You just need to find out the name of the school and we'll do the rest.
CHARLIE:	I know, but it's tough to flip and turn on him like this.
ZOEY:	*Excuse me?* I, along with everyone else in this room, was under the impression that you had *already* flipped and turned on him.
CHARLIE:	That was before I was being put up to *single-handedly* messing up his future!
ZOEY:	JOSH DOESN'T DESERVE A FUTURE.
CHARLIE:	TWO WRONGS DON'T MAKE A RIGHT.
ZOEY:	OH there are a *lot* more than "two wrongs" in the equation right now.
LEAH:	Charlie.
CHARLIE:	THAT'S NOT WHAT I MEANT.
LEAH:	*Charlie.*
CHARLIE:	WHAT.
LEAH:	… I understand if you don't want to do it. I get it. It's totally fine.
CHARLIE:	… It's just hard.
LEAH:	It's a lot to ask.

PIPER: We wouldn't be asking you if we didn't think you were capable.

LEAH: *(To PIPER.)* It's fine. Charlie. Seriously, it's okay. *(To PIPER and ZOEY.)* There's gotta be something else we can do that doesn't put her in this position.

PIPER: *(To LEAH.)* Are you sure?

LEAH: I don't want to hurt Charlie like this.

CHARLIE: I'll do it.

LEAH: —what?

CHARLIE: I'll do it. I'll talk to Josh.

LEAH: …Thanks.

                Shift. JOSH and CHARLIE are solving a jigsaw puzzle.

JOSH: Got another one.

CHARLIE: I thought we said we were gonna stop announcing it whenever we solve one.

JOSH: Shit, right.

CHARLIE: Ooh, got one! … oh shit.

JOSH: Whatever. I say, successes are worth celebrating.

CHARLIE: Is finding one piece a success?

JOSH: A small one.

                They keep working. JOSH is focussed on the puzzle, CHARLIE is focussed more on JOSH. In the next moment, CHARLIE is more focussed on the puzzle while JOSH is more focussed on CHARLIE. She gets up and goes to the kitchen.

CHARLIE: Want a beer?

JOSH: Sure.

CHARLIE: Sorry I didn't go to your birthday thing.

JOSH: Hey, that's okay.

CHARLIE: *(Returning with beers.)* What'd you end up doing?

JOSH: Oh I just hung out with Ethan and Tommy.

CHARLIE: Well, happy belated.

JOSH: Yeah, thanks. Man... twenty-three... weird how fast time flies.

CHARLIE: And how much things change.

JOSH: Yeah.

CHARLIE: Speaking of which, I got you a birthday present.

JOSH: If this is another pair of earrings, I'm still not gonna get my ears pierced.

CHARLIE: *(Pulling out a present, wrapped nicely.)* It's not, but I still think you could pull that off.

JOSH: All right, let's see...

> He opens it and pulls out a tweed sport coat, complete with elbow patches.

JOSH: What's this?

CHARLIE: All the best teachers have "The Jacket." I bought it at Piper's work a while ago and I was gonna save it to be a graduation present, but I figured why wait?

JOSH: This is so good. You really didn't have to, though.

CHARLIE: I wanted to. Because you love teaching. And you'd make a great teacher.

JOSH: Thanks, man.

CHARLIE: Well, go on! Put it on!

JOSH: Right, right. *(He does.)*

CHARLIE: Man, you're such a teacher in that.

JOSH: I feel like Mr. Jensen.

CHARLIE: Bless that man, I would not have survived English 30 without him.

JOSH: SAME. Dude, this is so good. And right before my last practicum too!

A moment. They focus back the puzzle.

JOSH: I think I'm almost done the green section.

CHARLIE: You got it last time, you'll get it again.

JOSH: I still can't believe you tore this apart.

CHARLIE: *(Laughing.)* Are you serious?

JOSH: *Hours* of our lives were put into this.

CHARLIE: Well, puzzles can only sit on the table for so many months before I start to feel like an annoying roommate.

JOSH: Speaking of those two…

CHARLIE: Oh, they're out.

JOSH: …Still nothing I can do to fix things with them?

CHARLIE: I don't really wanna get into it now.

JOSH: I just mean—

CHARLIE: Not now. Let's just hang out today, okay? Like we said we would. No drama.

JOSH: No drama.

CHARLIE: Deal.

JOSH: Thank god! 'Cause I just can't escape it. Like, everywhere I go, I'm like "Who knows?", "Who's out to get me?" Dude, I was so glad you texted me.

CHARLIE: I just figured we might as well put the whole thing behind us and move on, right?

            Throughout the following, CHARLIE chugs her beer.

JOSH: Yes! Exactly. I'm so glad you realized that 'cause like, it was killing me not being able to just like, hang out like normal and I was starting to get really worried. Especially if you weren't on my side, right? And honestly, I learned my lesson. For real. I don't wanna hurt anyone ever again.

CHARLIE: *(Putting down her beer bottle.)* Let's smoke something!

JOSH: … okay, sure!

CHARLIE: Just 'cause, like you said, we might as well just have fun, right?

JOSH: Right, yeah!

CHARLIE: Yeah!

            CHARLIE starts getting her pipe and lighter. Throughout the following, she avoids eye contact.

JOSH: Am I gonna get in shit when Zoey and Piper come home?

CHARLIE: They won't be home for a while.

JOSH: How do you know?

CHARLIE: I know everything. The only thing I don't know is where my lighter got to... How's school? How's that going?

JOSH: School? Oh it's uhh, it's good! Midterms are wild and stuff, but I'm so pumped for my practicum!

CHARLIE: Where did my lighter go?

JOSH: Is it in your purse?

CHARLIE: I don't think so.

JOSH: You should check your purse.

CHARLIE: It wouldn't be in my bag because I took it out this morning to lend it to Zoey...

JOSH: *(Checking her purse.)* Oh my god...

CHARLIE: Like, I gave it to Zoey over here, and then she took it outside, and then—

JOSH: *(He finds it.)* Here it is.

CHARLIE: Oh.

JOSH: Every time.

CHARLIE: Shut up. *(Starting to load the pipe.)* What were we talking about?

JOSH: Something with school—oh right, my practicum!

CHARLIE: Right. That.

JOSH:	Yeah man! And I finally found out which school I'm teaching at and I seriously lucked out. Oh and I forgot to tell you what happened with Kevin the other day—
CHARLIE:	So which school? Like, what's the name?
JOSH:	Oh, right. Louise McKinney!
CHARLIE:	*(Passing him the pipe and the lighter.)* Here, start it off.
JOSH:	*(Taking the pipe.)* Sure, thanks. And yeah, I think they call it "McKinney" for short.
CHARLIE:	Piper went there.
JOSH:	Really?
CHARLIE:	Yeah. Just a few years ago…

JOSH takes a drag then passes it to CHARLIE.

CHARLIE:	*(Taking it.)* Thanks.
JOSH:	I thought you were gonna try to cut back.
CHARLIE:	I was. But it's, uhm… it's stressful times right now.
JOSH:	With midterms and everything?
CHARLIE:	Yeah. Midterms.
JOSH:	You got this, man. It'll all pay off eventually. Or at least that's what I tell myself whenever I'm doing something I don't wanna do.
CHARLIE:	Yeah. This is all for the better in the long run.
JOSH:	Exactly.
CHARLIE:	In the big picture.

The next day. ZOEY enters from the kitchen with a bag of arugula which she munches on throughout the scene. She speaks to PIPER, who is in the other room.

ZOEY:

Piper, I never *actually* liked Dallas. Like, *so what* if we're not a thing anymore, or whatever we were...

PIPER enters from her room, looking a bit more spiffy than usual.

PIPER:

Then why'd you buy a beta fish with him?

ZOEY:

It's just a fish! What are you all dressed up for?

PIPER:

I was gonna go walk around Richmond. Wanna come?

ZOEY:

What brought this on?

PIPER:

Nothing.

ZOEY:

Wanna wear my jean jacket with that?

PIPER:

The one you *stole*?

ZOEY:

What difference does it make?

PIPER:

I don't know, it's just funny. Like, for someone who went to law school, you sure like to break them.

ZOEY:

I did not go to law school.

PIPER:

First year still counts.

ZOEY:

Everyone goes through an Elle Woods phase. Mine just lasted a long time.

PIPER:

Oh come on, you actually wanted to be a prosecutor. And like, if that's what you still wanna do, you should go for it.

ZOEY: It's not what I *still wanna do,* thank you very much.

PIPER: But if you *did* —

ZOEY: I DON'T.

PIPER: WHOA, chill, I just said—

ZOEY: University is a messed-up institution where rapists get elected as student body presidents and I'm not going back.

PIPER: He graduated! You wouldn't even have to see him. Plus it's not *entirely* bullshit.

ZOEY: Really? 'Cause somehow there are still a bunch of guys strutting around that campus who have literally forced themselves inside us while I'm sitting over here with a criminal record for stealing lipstick from Shoppers Drug Mart.

PIPER: Well, if you think the system's so messed up, why'd you make Leah go report Josh?

ZOEY: Don't you have somewhere to be?

PIPER: Yeah, I just gotta brush my teeth.

ZOEY: *Well, why don't you go do that then.*

PIPER: *(Heading to the bathroom.)* God...

> *ZOEY angrily munches on her arugula. It's not satisfying enough. She swaps it out for a bag of chips, sitting on the coffee table. She eats more chips. She goes to her room. She comes back wearing the jean jacket that she stole and sewed patches on. She resumes her business eating chips. Still not satisfying enough. She reaches into*

the couch cushion and pulls out a pack of cigarettes. She takes one out. She thinks about it. She can't help it.

ZOEY: (*To PIPER in the other room.*) I'm going for a walk.

ZOEY hurries out the front door with a single cigarette. Piper enters with a toothbrush.

PIPER: What did you say?

She looks out the window and watches ZOEY walk away. She notices the pack of cigarettes. Suddenly, LEAH bursts through the front door, out of breath.

PIPER: Oh. Hi.

LEAH: Hey.

PIPER: ... everything okay?

LEAH: Yeah. Just uh... just wanted to come over... to show you what I wrote.

PIPER: Oh. Okay...?

LEAH: Sorry, I was just... I was fine but then I just— well I took a shortcut 'cause—

PIPER: It's fine.

LEAH: I wanted to show you the letter I wrote but I passed his passed his passed his uhh his place. I passed his place and then I—

PIPER: Passed whose place? What letter?

CHARLIE comes home.

CHARLIE: Ugh, sorry I took so long getting home. Still wanna watch *Corpse Bride* or—oh. *(Sees LEAH.)* … what's up?

PIPER: She just got here. And she has something to show us but something happened on the way here?

LEAH: No, no nothing happened. I just got really scared and like, couldn't stop thinking about what would like—no, doesn't matter.

PIPER: You said you passed someone's house on the way here?

LEAH: Yeah, I wanted to get here faster so I cut down 59th and then I forgot he lives in that building.

PIPER: Who?

LEAH: / Josh.

CHARLIE: Josh. You passed Josh's place on the way here and started spiralling?

LEAH: *(Nodding.)* And then I got really paranoid. I don't know, I kept thinking someone would jump out of the bushes and stab me or something. Which is stupid, but still. And then I ran and then I lost track of where I was and then—

PIPER: Want a Red Bull?

CHARLIE: Just wait, Piper.

PIPER goes to the kitchen.

CHARLIE: I'm really sorry that happened. It must've been really scary.

LEAH: I feel like an idiot.

CHARLIE: You're not an idiot. You're here. You're with us. He's not here.

LEAH: Like, I just kept looking at his place and it all came flooding back then it was like I could feel him on me and I could like taste a taste a taste a cigarette and then—

PIPER: *(From the kitchen.)* Was that a "yes" to the Red Bull?

CHARLIE: Hold *on*, Piper.

LEAH: *(To PIPER.)* Why the hell not!

CHARLIE: You were saying? Something about tasting cigarettes?

LEAH: Oh yeah, it's so dumb but like, I just wanna go slap him in the face or kick him in the balls or something. Make him hurt too. And I've never felt like that before and I'm just so mad because he's just *fine*. And that's so dumb because nothing is right it's all a big ugly mess it's a mess Charlie it's such a big goddamn mess!

PIPER: *(Passing LEAH a Red Bull.)* Here.

LEAH: ...do you ever want to not be a girl? Like... walk down the street at night without freaking out, not get interrupted all the time, not get touched all the time? I just mean—all this hurting...it's eating me inside. How does everyone in the group carry this with them all the time?

CHARLIE: We just do. We just move forward and carry it with us—

LEAH: But you guys are all fine! You're so focused on school, and you guys have jobs, and Zoey's always out—

CHARLIE: Listen, don't take Zoey for more than what she is. And as for me, I take *two* classes at school. And honestly I'm probably gonna drop out because I don't want to pay an institution that lets stuff like this slide.

LEAH: So you get what I mean, then? About not wanting to be a girl?

CHARLIE: Well. It sucks feeling silenced. But I think girls are pretty cool. And I think girls are strong. And if I were a guy, or if I hadn't been so *damaged* by a guy, I wouldn't have this fire under my ass fuelling me to *fight* for what's right. And I don't know about you, but I want to see the day we make a change.

PIPER: ...I kind of want to see that, too.

LEAH: That reminds me, I came here to read you what I wrote. I haven't sent it yet, but I wrote the email! 'Cause I decided to finally *do* something, you know?

            LEAH passes her phone to PIPER, who starts reading the email. ZOEY comes home.

CHARLIE: Where were you?

ZOEY: I went for a walk. *(Notices LEAH.)* When did you get here? Are you okay?

LEAH: I'm fine, I just came to show you guys the email I wrote.

ZOEY: You did it? You sent it?

LEAH: Not yet. Still not sure who to send it to.

ZOEY: Well, Charlie found out which school we need to send it to, right?

CHARLIE:	Yeah. I talked to Josh.
PIPER:	Leah, I think it's awesome. Really clear.
ZOEY:	*(Grabbing LEAH's phone.)* Let me see.
LEAH:	If you guys think it's good, we could send it like, right now.
PIPER:	Charlie, which school is it? I'll google their email.
CHARLIE:	The school? It's uhh…
ZOEY:	Don't tell me you forgot the name of the school.
CHARLIE:	Aren't you busy reading Leah's email?
ZOEY:	You know the name of the school. Spit it out.
PIPER:	Charlie, do you not wanna do it?
LEAH:	Come on! We're so close!
ZOEY:	Yeah!
CHARLIE:	Kay, this isn't a *game*.
ZOEY:	Who said anything about a game?
CHARLIE:	Nothing—no one. It's just not *fun* for me, okay?
ZOEY:	This is serious. This is what the group is for.
CHARLIE:	Well "the group" backfired on us, now didn't it?
ZOEY:	*"Backfired"?*
PIPER:	Remember the big picture, Charlie.
ZOEY:	Do you want to do it or not?
CHARLIE:	No, I do. Just…

ZOEY:	He raped Leah!
LEAH:	Kay, stop shouting that.
ZOEY:	You haven't heard me shout!
CHARLIE:	Zoey, how would you feel if you were plotting against your best friend of six years?
ZOEY:	I'd get over it!
PIPER:	Guys!
ZOEY:	It's not that hard! Charlie: That. Guy. Is. Toxic. He raped Leah, he made out with Gabby while she was drunk, he's assaulted Quinta, and Haley, and Paige and PROBABLY MORE. So why in the name of holy fuck are you making it so hard to do the right thing here?
CHARLIE:	Can we just PLEASE wait and let me *think*?
ZOEY:	I'M SICK OF WAITING. I've been waiting for, for years. YEARS, Charlie! We've all been waiting for a signal or SOMETHING to tell us that it's time to fight. It's *our* turn to win! Hell, even *Piper's* down to do this.
PIPER:	Not unless we're all in agreement.
ZOEY:	MY GOD GUYS. Are we a team or not?
CHARLIE:	I was about to ask you the same question.
LEAH:	Charlie, I'm really sorry. Should I not have—
ZOEY:	Stop apologizing, Leah.
LEAH:	Well I just want you to stop yelling because when you yell it makes everybody yell to try to match you / and then it's just a big yelling match of yelling and yelling stresses me out so just please stop YELLING.

ZOEY: I'm only / yelling because I don't understand why everyone is so content to sit around and talk about a plan and not fucking put it into action!

PIPER: Oh, would you two just shut up for five fucking seconds and realize that we are supposed to be in agreement on this before we EXPOSE HIM?

CHARLIE: *(Banging the table.) HEYYYYY!!!* Everybody calm the fuck down.

LEAH: I'm sorry.

ZOEY: I'm not.

PIPER: Charlie—

CHARLIE: I'm not ready to do this. I never will be because…well, six years. You can't cut someone out of your life who has been by your side for that long. And it's hard because the whole reason I made this group is because a boy did something awful to me. And aside from the group, Josh is the person who helped me rebuild after that and and and—so now to turn around and and and to flip it on *him* and…and I'm *trying* really hard to come to terms with the fact that this was a waste of six years. Or maybe it wasn't, I don't know. But what would you do, Zoey, if you were me?

ZOEY: Simple, I would—

CHARLIE: You know, he was the first person I opened up to about what Austin did to me back in high school. I confided in him and I cried in his arms and he let me stay at his place when my parents kicked me out before I even met you guys. And he never once asked for anything in return. And he was the one who convinced me to try going to university part-time, and he was the one who tutored me in Math 30 so I could get my high school diploma. And he was the first person in my life who said "Tell me what happened" that I actually listened to. So yes, he is my friend. And yes, he's done some awful things. But...if I cut him out of my life, it will be because the thought of him making so many other people feel the way I felt in high school after my stupid ex-asshole-boyfriend took everything from me makes me feel like I'm being punched in the gut from the inside. So I'll proofread the letter or whatever, and I'll give you the name of the school but I won't enjoy it. And I won't relish in it. And I won't ever be enthusiastic about it because that's just not in the cards for me, okay?

ZOEY: ... read her the letter.

LEAH: "To Whom It May Concern:

My name is Leah Madison, I am seventeen years old and I am writing to warn you about the possibility of my abuser getting the opportunity to teach your students. Joshua Hansen is in his final year of his Education degree and about to do his final practicum at your school. Joshua Hansen has also sexually assaulted five women in the past six years. If you need proof, he was reported after four of the five offences. Please feel free to contact me with any questions regarding where to look into these reports. I am one of the survivors. Joshua Hansen raped me in September while I was severely intoxicated and hardly capable of walking.

I am contacting you out of concern for the safety of your students. They should not be taught by someone with a recorded history of harming women. As a rape survivor, I do not wish for any of your students—regardless of gender—to experience what I have had to go through.

Please contact me with any questions.

Sincerely, Leah Madison"

A moment. They all look at CHARLIE.

LEAH: What do you think?

CHARLIE: … I think you're really brave. And I'm sorry he did that to you.

PIPER: *(Opening her laptop.)* We just need you to tell us which school to send it to.

CHARLIE: McKinney.

PIPER: Whoa. Actually?

LEAH: What's so special about that?

PIPER: That's my old high school…okay, let's see. "Contact"…okay here it is. Leah, wanna write this down?

             LEAH types the email address into her phone.

LEAH: All right… do you guys think this'll work?

PIPER: It's worth a shot.

ZOEY: You're doing the right thing, Leah.

LEAH: Okay. You guys want in on this?

ZOEY: What, we all send it?

LEAH:	Yeah. Come on. Together.

LEAH puts her phone on the coffee table. ZOEY, PIPER and LEAH each put a finger on the "Send" button. CHARLIE hesitates, then follows.

ZOEY:	Charlie. You've got us.
CHARLIE:	I know.
LEAH:	On three. One… two… three.

They click. No one knows what to do now.

PIPER:	Anybody want a drink?
ZOEY:	/ Yep!
CHARLIE:	Yes.
PIPER:	We could go to Rich Rat? It's probably still Happy Hour.
LEAH:	I think I actually wanna just go home if that's cool.
ZOEY:	Want us to walk you home?
LEAH:	Sure, yeah. That would be nice.
ZOEY:	Charlie, you coming?
CHARLIE:	… what? Oh. Nah, I'm pretty tired.
ZOEY:	Okay. Well… call us if you need anything.
PIPER:	Yeah. Rich Rat isn't far.
CHARLIE:	Yeah. For sure.
PIPER:	And hey, when I get home, *Corpse Bride?*
CHARLIE:	Yeah, maybe.

> *PIPER, ZOEY, and LEAH start to head out.*

LEAH: Didn't you *just* watch that one?

PIPER: No.

ZOEY: She watched it last week.

PIPER: Not last week.

ZOEY: That was SO last week, I remember.

PIPER: Bye, Charlie!

ZOEY: Yeah, see ya!

CHARLIE: Bye.

> *PIPER and ZOEY exit. LEAH hangs back a moment.*

LEAH: Thanks, Charlie.

CHARLIE: Don't mention it. Seriously.

> *LEAH exits. CHARLIE stays put for a moment. She did it! It's over now. She takes a breath and tries to decide what to do next. She gets the bong and starts looking around for a lighter. A knock at the door. Before she can even go to answer it, JOSH opens the door. CHARLIE freezes. JOSH is wearing a big hoodie and his hair is messy. Throughout the following, JOSH often has his eyes cast downward.*

CHARLIE: What are you doing here?

JOSH: Just stopping by. I was gonna see if you wanted to hang out.

CHARLIE: Why didn't you just text me?

JOSH:	Because you're not answering my texts…
CHARLIE:	Well, maybe you should take the hint.
JOSH:	I just couldn't take it anymore and—
CHARLIE:	You can't just walk into people's houses.
JOSH:	Right. I know. I know that. I do…. know that. But well, I just figured—
CHARLIE:	Doesn't matter.
JOSH:	All good?
CHARLIE:	Yeah. I'm just—I don't know, I'm just startled.
JOSH:	Sorry. I just…it's just that I'm so used to just walking in that—sorry.
CHARLIE:	What do you want?
JOSH:	… Look, if this is a bad time, I'll just head home, it's fine.
CHARLIE:	Well, no, it's just. Nothing.

> JOSH stays put by the door. He can read CHARLIE's face.

JOSH:	You all good?
CHARLIE:	Yup.
JOSH:	Okay… *(Looks around the room.)* You put the puzzle away.
CHARLIE:	I got rid of it.
JOSH:	Oh.
CHARLIE:	It was taking up too much space in here.
JOSH:	All good…

Another awkward stalemate. JOSH is doing the math in his head.

JOSH: You sure everything's cool?

CHARLIE: ...yeah.

JOSH: You know, I ran into Piper on campus last week. She was sketching in the quad.

CHARLIE: Yeah, I don't know what happened but she just got this spike of confidence.

JOSH: Is she home?

CHARLIE: No, they all left. We're going to Rich Rat. I would invite you but they, uhm... they probably don't want to see you.

JOSH: Do *you* even want to see me? (*Nothing from CHARLIE.*) I uhm, I wanted to tell you... I stopped by earlier last week. Piper was home and—

CHARLIE: I know.

JOSH: Oh. Okay.

CHARLIE: You didn't seriously think that you could come to my house and talk to my roommate about me and have her not tell me, did you?

JOSH: It was a long shot, I guess.

CHARLIE: Piper said you wanted to know if you were losing me.

JOSH: Well, yeah. I did. But then we hung out like normal and I figured—

CHARLIE: I thought I could do it but now I'm not so sure. Hang out like normal and stuff.

JOSH:	We can. I told you, that'll never *ever* happen again.
CHARLIE:	No, listen. I invited you over to hang out the other day because I was actually—
JOSH:	We can put this behind us.
CHARLIE:	*(That one stings.)* You're joking, right?
JOSH:	Well why'd you act like everything was fine the other day?
CHARLIE:	"Put this behind us"–are you kidding me?
JOSH:	…Look, you didn't wanna talk about it before but I wanted to say I'm sorry.
CHARLIE:	I know you are.
JOSH:	Not just to Leah and Gabby and Haley and them, but to you.
CHARLIE:	*I know.*
JOSH:	I know you know, I just feel the need to keep saying it.
CHARLIE:	We've been over this, it's not going to fix anything.
JOSH:	Well, since I can't fix anything I just want you to know that I'm really genuinely sincerely sorry for what I did and I wish I could go back in time and—
CHARLIE:	*Josh, please.*
JOSH:	Sorry!
CHARLIE:	This hurts a lot, you know.
JOSH:	I know.

CHARLIE: *(Laughs slightly.)* See that right there. *That's* why this hurts. You *know* how much this hurts all those girls because you've *seen it*, and you let me open up to you about it for years.

JOSH: Exactly, I know how I made them feel and it kills me, Charlie, you have no idea.

CHARLIE: No, it doesn't.

JOSH: I can't sleep, okay? I haven't slept in in in I don't know, but I just—no GOD that doesn't matter it's not about me it's not it's it's about you THEM it's about them. But it's about you *and* them, GOD see I just, I just picture them crying the way you cried to me and it crushes me. And I don't know what to do, you know? It follows me everywhere, and and I'm scared, Charlie. I'm fucking terrified. I don't wanna be this but it's like I already am and I just… yeah it crushes me!

CHARLIE: *No, it doesn't.*

JOSH: Yes, it does.

CHARLIE: No! It doesn't "crush you" and it doesn't "fucking kill you" because if it did then none of this would have happened and you would have stopped when they wanted you to stop and you would have backed off when they wanted you to back off and you wouldn't have brought Leah back to your apartment and you wouldn't have had sex with her!

JOSH: I'M SORRY, OKAY.

CHARLIE: I DON'T GIVE A SHIT, JOSH. YOU *RUINED* PEOPLE. YOU RUINED MY FRIENDS. YOU RUINED *ME!*

CHARLIE begins to hit JOSH repeatedly. He is stronger than she is. He does not hit back. He grabs her arms and holds them out to stop her. She starts to kick him instead.

CHARLIE: You ruined everybody—everything. / Gabby...Haley...Paige...Quinta, and this one's for Leah, and you also ruined me and Zoey and Piper and me.

JOSH: Charlie—Charlie, hey, stop it. Calm down. *Calm down.* Charlie—Charlie— *Charlie!*

He pushes her off. They look at each other. A couple deep breaths. Suddenly, CHARLIE goes towards him again. JOSH gets ready to block another hit. Instead, CHARLIE hugs him tightly, and finally breaks. He hugs her back.

CHARLIE: It's out of my hands now.

JOSH: I know.

CHARLIE: But I'm not against it either.

JOSH: I know.

CHARLIE: And I can barely look at you.

JOSH: I know.

CHARLIE: *(Pulls away.)* Then how come you did it, Joshy?

JOSH: I didn't know.

CHARLIE: How could you not know?

JOSH: I just didn't realize...but it all just happened, and I can't wish it back.

CHARLIE: I don't know what's gonna happen to you now.

JOSH: Well, your friends are probably gonna report me or something, right?

CHARLIE: Worse than that.

JOSH: What do you mean?

CHARLIE: (*Urgent, almost a whisper.*) Leah's seventeen.

                         JOSH takes a couple steps back. Checkmate.

CHARLIE: … I think this is it, Joshy.

JOSH: No.

CHARLIE: It's out of my hands.

JOSH: Stop saying that—I'm not gonna listen to this.

CHARLIE: We can't change anything.

JOSH: (*Grabbing her shoulders.*) No, no no no no no, Charlie, listen to me.

CHARLIE: I can't listen to you.

JOSH: We can mend this. This is not "bye" forever. It'll just take time.

CHARLIE: No, we can't. We won't. You're a completely different person to me now.

JOSH: I'll find a way to fix it.

CHARLIE: There's no way to fix it.

JOSH: …well dude, I—

CHARLIE: I can't help you.

JOSH: So we're not friends anymore? Just like that?

CHARLIE: I guess so.

JOSH: Friends like us don't just say goodbye like this, Charlie.

CHARLIE doesn't know what to say. JOSH doesn't know what to do.

Shift. Spotlight on ZOEY as she makes a post in "Tell Us What Happened."

ZOEY: Hey everyone! Charlie, Piper, and I are just trying to figure out roughly how many people will be joining us for the "Tell Us What Happened" Three Year Anniversary party. It'll be so awesome to get everyone together! If you haven't already RSVP'd in the Facebook event, please do that. Hope to see you all soon!

Shift. One month later. PIPER works on a banner for the "Tell Us What Happened" party. LEAH sits on the couch, scrolling through the ringtone options on PIPER's phone.

LEAH: What about this one?

A ringtone briefly plays.

PIPER: No.

LEAH: Okay… how about "Constellation"?

Another ringtone briefly plays.

PIPER: Too electronic.

LEAH: This one?

Another ringtone briefly plays.

PIPER: Too boring.

Another one.

PIPER: Too electronic. And boring.

LEAH: I still don't get what's wrong with "Smooth Wave," I like it.

                "Smooth Wave" plays.

PIPER: It's just too *(Makes an obscure arm gesture.)*—

LEAH: What does *(Arm gesture.)* mean?

PIPER: I don't know. Maybe it's just / too electronic.

LEAH: Too electronic.

                ZOEY and CHARLIE burst in laughing and carrying shopping bags.

CHARLIE: Come ON, you totally owe me!

ZOEY: It wasn't him! He's got super dark hair, remember?

CHARLIE: You owe me five bucks! Or just buy me a beer sometime and we'll call it even.

PIPER: Call it even for what?

ZOEY: Kay, so we were at the mall, right? And Charlie was *convinced* that she saw Luke Matichuk working at the pretzel kiosk—

PIPER: That doesn't make any sense though because—

ZOEY: Kay, *right?*

PIPER: — yeah because Luke definitely moved to Quebec for school. Like, that's the whole reason you two broke up, isn't it?

ZOEY: And THEN, she's all "Go rekindle your old flames" and I'm like "first of all, no way, second of all, it's NOT HIM" and she's like "yes it / is, it's totally him!"—

CHARLIE:	IT WAS TOTALLY HIM.
ZOEY:	And THEN, Charlie full-on *goes up* and BUYS A PRETZEL FROM THE PRETZEL KIOSK just so she can hear his voice.
CHARLIE:	I'd know it if I heard it!
ZOEY:	And we bet five bucks on whether or not it was him. And now she thinks I owe her five bucks because she thinks this random blond dude's *customer service voice* sounded like Luke Matichuk.
CHARLIE:	It WAS Luke Matichuk!
ZOEY:	Luke isn't blond!
PIPER:	Maybe he dyed it.
CHARLIE:	I'm pulling up his Instagram.
LEAH:	*(To ZOEY.)* Why didn't *you* go buy a pretzel from him, too?
ZOEY:	'Cause I didn't want a pretzel! Charlie didn't even want a pretzel!
CHARLIE:	Found him! Found him found him found him!
PIPER:	And? Is he blond now?
CHARLIE:	BAM. A selfie posted nine days ago.
ZOEY:	Okay, so he dyed his hair. That's not to say he works at the pretzel kiosk, though.
CHARLIE:	Good thing this selfie was taken from INSIDE THE PRETZEL KIOSK. *(Showing ZOEY her phone.)* Look, he's in uniform and everything. I was right!

ZOEY:	*(Shrugging and pulling out her wallet.)* Whatever. You win, then.
PIPER:	*(Taking CHARLIE's phone.)* Can I see his profile?
CHARLIE:	Just don't like any of his photos.
PIPER:	I won't—oh shit, you're getting a call.
CHARLIE:	From who?
PIPER:	*(Passing CHARLIE's phone back.)* Oh shit.
CHARLIE:	Oh…. fuck…
LEAH:	Who is it?
CHARLIE:	Janet.
ZOEY:	Whoa, what?
LEAH:	Who's Janet?
CHARLIE:	/ Josh's mom.
PIPER:	/ Josh's mom.
ZOEY:	Josh's mom.
LEAH:	Oh fuck.
ZOEY:	She probably just wants to ask Charlie what happened when she and Leah met with the school board last week.
PIPER:	I bet she's pissed at us.
ZOEY:	You can handle it, Charlie. You're tight with Janet.
PIPER:	Still though, you don't have to answer that.
LEAH:	Yeah. Don't answer if you don't want to.
CHARLIE:	Well, I can't just ghost her…

They all stare at the phone until it stops ringing. LEAH tries to change the energy.

LEAH: Uhm. SO. Check out the awesome banner Piper's making for the party tomorrow!

ZOEY: Yeah! It's looking awesome. We bought some glitter for it on the way home.

PIPER: Great! Yeah, I'm gonna put a border on it if you guys wanna help with that.

CHARLIE's phone rings again. They all stop.

ZOEY: Is it—

CHARLIE: Yep.

ZOEY: Shit. I mean, you might as well answer it. How bad could it be?

CHARLIE: I'm gonna have to tell her, aren't I?

PIPER: Unless Josh told her why the school board keeps trying to get a hold of him.

CHARLIE: *(Taking a deep breath.)* I mean, if I can tell Josh he's a sex offender, surely I can tell his mom, right?

ZOEY: That's the spirit!

CHARLIE: *(Answering the phone.)* Hello?

Throughout the following, the other girls start to unpack the glitter and take out paintbrushes.

CHARLIE: Yeah, hey Janet. Sorry I missed your call there, I just got home from the farmers' market...

Oh that's sweet of you, no I yeah I just missed your first call...

Good, good, I'm good, yeah. Busy. But good...

Is everything okay...?

Told me about what?

No, I'm home. I'm with my roommates...

Okay...

Okay... are you okay? You sound.........

(To the girls.) She's crying so hard she can't talk. She's passing me over to his dad... guys, it sounds really bad.

ZOEY:	Well, it is kind of shocking.
CHARLIE:	No like, it sounds *bad* bad.
ZOEY:	Well, hang up if you want.
CHARLIE:	I'm not gonna—hi Rob. Hey. Is Janet okay?

Shocked about what?

No, I haven't spoken to him for a while actually...

> PIPER *drops what she's doing and stares at* CHARLIE. ZOEY *and* LEAH *exchange a look but keep crafting.*

CHARLIE: No, I didn't hear anything from him last night... we haven't been talking at all actually...

I have no idea where he was, I haven't seen him in...

Why? What's going on?

...*What?*

No. No. No no, you're not serious.

No…

Oh my god…

> ZOEY and LEAH freeze and look at
> CHARLIE. Throughout the following,
> PIPER, ZOEY, and LEAH keep exchanging
> looks and staring at CHARLIE, otherwise
> they are frozen.

CHARLIE: Oh my god…

What so he just… no he would've come to me
if he were… he would've told me if he was
feeling like— like if he was gonna…

No…

He would've told me.

No, he didn't—he wouldn't. He was okay—
this wasn't…oh my god…

But he was okay… he was—he was—
wouldn't he have…

I gotta go.

(Hanging up.) I'm gonna be sick.

> CHARLIE throws her phone at the couch
> and runs to the washroom to vomit. The
> girls sit in shock.

LEAH: Did he…

ZOEY: We don't know that.

LEAH: But it sounds like he—

ZOEY: *We don't know that.*

LEAH: Well, why else would she—

PIPER: Guys. I think he did.

ZOEY: No. No, he didn't.

PIPER: Zoey. Just be quiet, okay.

> *The girls sit in front of the art project and wait for CHARLIE. CHARLIE slowly re-enters.*

LEAH: Charlie—

> *PIPER puts a hand on LEAH's shoulder to stop her from talking. The following moves slowly.*

CHARLIE: ……… Josh hung himself last night.

> *No one knows what to do. No one knows what to say.*

CHARLIE: They found him in his place this morning. Had to beat the door down.

LEAH: No.

PIPER: Charlie…

ZOEY: Oh my god.

PIPER: Holy fuck…

CHARLIE: They wanted me to be the first to know.

LEAH: No…

ZOEY: Charlie, I'm so sorry.

PIPER: Oh my god no no no no no…

CHARLIE: They told me to call them if I ever need them for anything or if I'm ever in trouble…they said they love me like a daughter.

PIPER: No no no no no…

LEAH:	Oh god, I didn't mean for—
CHARLIE:	It's not your fault.
LEAH:	But I didn't mean—I didn't mean—

PIPER puts a hand on LEAH's shoulder to stop her from talking.

CHARLIE:	You guys can put the glitter away.

The girls sit in shock. The Clubhouse is silent.

End of Play.